MW00655843

THE MASTERY MANUAL

A Life-Changing Guide for Personal and Professional Greatness

ROBIN SHARMA

JAICO PUBLISHING HOUSE

Ahmedabad Bangalore Chennai
Delhi Hyderabad Kolkata Mumbai

Published by Jaico Publishing House
A-2 Jash Chambers, 7-A Sir Phirozshah Mehta Road
Fort, Mumbai - 400 001
jaicopub@jaicobooks.com
www.jaicobooks.com

© Robin Sharma

Published in arrangement with
Sharma Leadership International Inc.
92 Scollard Street, 2nd Floor
Toronto, ON M5R 1G2, Canada

To be sold only in India, Bangladesh, Bhutan,
Pakistan, Nepal, Sri Lanka and the Maldives.

THE MASTERY MANUAL
ISBN 978-81-8495-408-1

First Jaico Impression: 2015
28th Jaico Impression: 2023

No part of this book may be reproduced or utilized in
any form or by any means, electronic or
mechanical including photocopying, recording or by any
information storage and retrieval system,
without permission in writing from the publishers.

Page design and layout: Rashmi Graphics, Mumbai

Printed by
Rashmi Graphics, Mumbai

Contents

Module: 1	Live Fully Now	5
Module: 2	What Makes an Elite Performer?	11
Module: 3	A Balanced Model for Success	19
Module: 4	Work As a Planet-Class Performance	23
Module: 5	The Steve Jobs Question	27
Module: 6	Small Daily Acts of Greatness (SDAG)	31
Module 7	Be a Life Long Learner	35
Module: 8	Destiny and Leadership	41
Module: 9	The Power of Your Associations	45
Module: 10	A Salute to My Heroes	51
Module: 11	Leadership Lesson of the Month	55
Module: 12	Leadership Through Fearlessness	61
Module: 13	The Many Forms of Wealth	67
Module: 14	The Power of Renewal	73
Module: 15	Create a Dream Book	77
Module: 16	5 Ways to Run Your Life Like an Elite Performer	85
Module: 17	Make Your Mark	91

Module: 18   I Challenge You to Play Your Biggest Game   95

Module: 19   The Eternal Quest for Happiness   101

Module: 20   The 5 Golden Disciplines of Life Mastery   107

Module: 21   Monumental Moments   111

Module: 22   Closing the Gap   115

Module: 23   Gratitude   121

Module: 24   A Devotion to Excellence   125

Module: 25   Reinvent Yourself   131

Module: 26   Are You Good?   135

Module: 27   Build a Great Day   141

Module: 28   What Makes an Elite Performer?   147

Module: 29   Build Your Awareness   153

Module: 30   Leadership Challenge   157

Module: 31   Lead Without Title   161

Module: 32   The Power of Perspective   165

Module: 33   The Human Side of Business   169

Module: 34   Renewal Through Travel   177

Module: 35   Life Wisdom to Enrich Your Path   181

Module: 36   The Need to Play Big   187

1

LIVE FULLY NOW

⊙

TOO MANY HUMAN beings postpone living. We say that
we will live our best lives when we have more time or when
we finish the pressing projects that are consuming us. We tell
those around us that we will be more loving and passionate when
things slow down. We promise ourselves that we will get into
world-class physical condition and eat healthier food when we
have a little bit more time. Yet, deep within us, each one of us
knows that there will never be a better time to live our biggest
life than now. And if not today, then when?

Most of us live as if we have all the time in the world. We put off
living and reaching for our highest and best. And yet, the days
slip into weeks, the weeks slip into months and the months slip
into years. Before you know it, your life will be over. And most

people, when they are on their deathbeds, have the same regrets: that they did not take enough risks, that they did not realize their highest personal potential. And they did not give more love.

There are no extra days. There are no meaningless days. This very day is the day that you can make a choice to stand for something higher and be the person you know in your heart you have always wanted to be. Today is the day you can make the decision to get into outstanding physical health or to be a genuine leader at work or to be more authentic as a human being or to take more risks and run towards your fears. To me, that's what leadership is all about. Seizing the moment and living your life as an example to others of what's possible for a human being to create. Keep thinking about what your best life will look like. As I share in my speeches and workshops: "with better awareness you can make better choices and when you make better choices, you will see better results."

INSPIRATIONAL QUOTES

"You don't drown by falling in the water; you drown by staying there."

Edwin Louis Cole

"After climbing a great hill, one only finds that there are many more hills to climb. I have taken a moment to rest, to steal a view of the glorious vista that surrounds me, to look back on the distance I have come. But I can only rest for a moment, for with freedom comes responsibilities, and I dare not linger, for my long walk has not yet ended."

Nelson Mandela

"If you do not shine as brightly as you have been destined to shine, you not only betray yourself – but the world is less of a place than it could have been."

Robin Sharma

6 WAYS TO ACHIEVE PERSONAL GREATNESS

1. Write out a 20-year plan for your professional as well as your personal life. Great companies ensure that they are governed by a well thought out mission, vision and value statement. A clear plan along with a statement of your most important values will allow you to make wiser choices which will lead to less failures.

2. Spend more time thinking. A client of mine has been one of India's most successful IT companies. One of their guiding philosophies is to encourage teammates to spend 1/3 of their time in contemplation. Most effective human beings think more than others. Think about what you want your life to represent. Think about how you can create more value. Think about what is not working in your life so you can make changes.

3. Get into balance. Striking a balance between your work and your personal life is not easy. It's an everyday challenge. But by working at it, your life will work much better. Schedule the time for exercise. Ensure that your family and friends get the priority they deserve. Take some time for yourself because when you feel better, you will be a source of positive energy to all those around you.

4. Take calculated risks. Every seven days, do something that makes you feel uncomfortable. The very thing that you are afraid to do is the thing that you should do first. Remember, on the other side of your fears, lives your growth.

5. Be more loving. Great teams are built by authentic leaders who are not afraid to speak truthfully and show kindness. This is not a sign of weakness, it is a sign of strength. Be loving, polite and compassionate to all those around you. This does not mean that you don't make the tough calls when you need to. What it really means is that you bring more of your humanity into your life.

6. Be different. Leaders, by definition, don't follow the crowd. Live life on your own terms. Listen to the values that are most true to you. Be creative. Remain an idealist.

The Value of your Reputation

My father once told me that it could take 30 years to build your reputation and yet it can be lost in 30 seconds. I truly believe that few things are as important as your good name. You can not put a price tag on getting your phone calls returned. And yet, so many people on the planet today suffer from short term thinking. They go for the cash grab in order to get the quick win. But, business success is all about relationship success. And that takes time. By underpromising and overdelivering, finishing what you start, being a great listener and delivering outrageous value for your clients, you will win their trust as well as their respect. That will promote your personal brand: your reputation. Guard your good name as one of your most cherished assets. Be impeccably honest and never do anything that will tarnish what you stand for. This will lead to a long career in business as well as a highly fulfilling life.

2

WHAT MAKES AN ELITE
PERFORMER?

⊙

LAST WEEK I spent 2 beautifully inspiring days with a group of senior executives representing Fortune 500 organizations, government agencies and entrepreneurial ventures. They had come together in a conference room at a Toronto hotel to participate in the The Elite Performers Series (EPS) which is a program I created about a year ago to help businesspeople lift their professional as well as their personal lives to all – new levels of success and significance. The breakthroughs I saw over the 2 days within that seminar room moved me deeply. It validated my belief that every single one of us has greatness within us – sometimes we just need a safe environment within which to access it and then let it shine.

As I got to know the participants in the program, it became more clear to me that each of us faces many of the same struggles. Each of us wants to find greater meaning in our lives. Each of us has dreams that we desire to fulfill. Each of us has fears that limit us. It also became clear to me that when we do not play our highest game at work and in our personal lives, we not only betray ourselves – we deny the people that we work with as well as the people that we serve the opportunity to have a piece of our magnificence. Indeed, the world will be a lesser place if each of us do not raise our standards and become the people we know in our hearts we are meant to become.

For your benefit, I have distilled a few of my thoughts on what makes an elite performer and offer them to you for your reflection:

1.   Elite performers play victor versus victim. As I travel around the world working with many diverse organizations as an executive coach, speaker and management consultant, I see many corporate cultures where there is a complete denial of personal responsibility. People blame others for what is not working within the organization. People point the finger at those around them for things gone wrong. But as I say in my book "Leadership Wisdom From The Monk Who Sold His Ferrari": "blaming others is nothing more than excusing yourself." Each of us has the power to create results. One person can change a corporate culture by making changes within her realm of influence. One person can begin behaving in new ways which leads those around him to do the same. In this way, a team can change, which influences a

culture to change which transforms an organization. If something is not working within your enterprise, use your power to effect the changes that you wish to see.

2. Elite performers focus on the worthy. Most people try to be all things to all people and, in so doing, achieve nothing. Elite performers have a laser-like focus on their highest priorities and an acute awareness of the best uses of their time. In fact, they build their whole lives around the activities that offer them the highest return on investment. They are good at saying no. They spend time each morning, during their Holy Hour planning and thinking strategically about what needs to be done during the day for them to play their highest games and be of most service.

3. Elite performers live their truth. Right now, this very moment, as you read this manual, you know deep in your heart what your professional as well as your personal life needs to look like in order for you to be living authentically. In this very moment, your heart knows what's right. Elite performers have articulated their personal philosophy along with their organizing principles and have the courage to live out that ideology each and every day of their lives. This gives them great power and promotes extraordinary levels of confidence because they are aware that they are being true to themselves.

4. Elite performers build human connections. Business is about relationships. Nothing is more important than building emotional engagement with your teammates, with your suppliers and with your customers. Competition in today's marketplace is not for "share of wallet", as many organizations falsely believe. Rather, the competition in today's marketplaces is for people's emotions. Show up fully in your relationships. Take the time to remember birthdays and write handwritten thank-you notes each week. Show people that you care. Open your heart to them and they will reward you with their loyalty as well as with their love.

5. Elite performers add outrageous value. I truly believe that we are rewarded in today's marketplace according to the value that we add. If you want to receive greater returns, add greater value. Give your customers and clients more value than they have any right to expect. Always underpromise and overdeliver. Stay up late into the night reflecting on how you can serve the people that you have the privilege to do business with and help them fulfill their dreams. Your career will begin to explode.

6. Elite performers are devoted to excellence. One of the things I focus on in a significant way during the 2 day Elite Performers Series program is a process that has been proven to help any employee become truly excellent in all that they do. To me, "excellence" is a beautiful word. Elite performers are constantly asking themselves the following question: "is the way that I'm showing up truly excellent and reflective of someone who is operating at a world-class standard?" We live in a world where mediocrity is the norm. When you truly dedicate yourself – no, devote yourself – to becoming excellent in the way that you think, and behave you stand out in a crowded marketplace. You show genuine leadership.

7. Elite performers deepen themselves. Nothing changes until you change. We live in an externally focused world where we buy into the notion that our lives will change when we make more money or get a better car or achieve more status. And yet, when we receive these things, we are left empty and unfulfilled. True success comes from inner success. Dedicate yourself to getting to know who you truly are. Reconnect with your brilliance. Walk towards your fears. Evaluate the quality of your life and what you want it to stand for. Reflect on the beliefs that are limiting you and ponder where you've picked them up from. The best investment you will ever make is investing in your best self.

Inspirational Quotes

"Encourage all your virtuous dispositions and exercise them whenever an opportunity arises, being assured that they will gain strength by exercise as a limb of the body does and that exercise will make them habitual."

Thomas Jefferson

"We are always getting ready to live, but never living."

Ralph Waldo Emerson

"Self-love is not only necessary and good, it is a pre-requisite for loving others."

Rollo May

"Today, be a little bolder. Reach a little higher. Be a little kinder. Be a bigger dreamer."

Robin Sharma

WHY KEEP A JOURNAL?

One of the practices that has changed my own life is the regular habit of journaling. In my speeches as well as in my coaching programs, I encourage and challenge participants to begin journaling in an effort to play their biggest games as human beings. Here is some of my thinking on why journaling is a powerful tool for personal discovery and elite performance:

1. Journaling allows you to take fuzzy thinking and distill it into precise language. Do you remember when you were in school and you thought you knew the material for an exam then met with a study group and realized, after discussing the material, that there were gaps in your understanding? Having a conversation about something forces you to find specific language for your thinking. Journaling is a conversation that you have with yourself. The more

learn from life. It allows you to let your days serve you. You become wiser each day. Journaling deepens commitment. The very act of writing things down deepens your resolve to make good things happen in your life. Try this today. Take 15 minutes to write about the day you want to create and the choices you are dedicated to making in order to create an excellent day. This simple act will allow you to be much more proactive rather than reactive as you live out the remaining hours of this day.

and see the work you do in a more lively, childlike way. Shift your mindset to see even the most mundane of tasks as an opportunity to stretch, grow and add value to your organization and its customers.

2. Reshape your environment. In my bestseller "Who Will Cry When You Die?", I suggest that we all create a pure environment, one that promotes healthy thoughts and peak performance on the playing field of life. The quality of your surroundings greatly affects the quality of your thinking. Ensure your workplace has inspiring posters and quotes in view, is uncluttered and clean and is a place where it is fun to work. Remember, the company that plays together stays together.

3. Reward "intelligent failures." I coined the term "intelligent failures" to remind us that great victories are always preceded by countless failures. Failure is the highway to success and making mistakes is the pathway to the big wins of business (and life). Rather than punishing those people on your team who take initiative but don't get it quite right the first time around, reward them for breaking out of the box and taking a beautiful risk. This will send a signal through your corporate culture: innovation matters!

4. Spend time in nature. Many readers of "The Monk Who Sold His Ferrari" have e-mailed me confirming that my suggestion of spending regular time in nature has given them million-dollar ideas that have improved both their professional and their

personal lives. Communing with nature gets you away from
the ringing phones and the flying faxes and connects you with
the higher part of you that is intuitive, wise and imaginative.
I always carry a dictaphone when I'm walking alone in the
woods, because the best thoughts come to me at these times, and
capturing them is crucial.

A Balanced Model for Success

◉

I HAVE STRUGGLED to find a balanced model for true
success in my life. At some times I have chased my goals and
heart's desires with all the force of a heat-seeking missile. At
other times, I have thought that the wisest way to act was in a
more gentle fashion and, after setting my intentions, letting life
unfold in a more organic way. I now think that the key is to have
a balanced approach for success. Too much striving is nothing
more than trying to control your destiny and force outcomes.
And simply stating your intentions (perhaps by telling them to
your friends or by listing them on a blank piece of paper) and
not moving them forward by dedicated action is nothing more
than spiritual apathy (which is based on fear). I believe that
achieving real success in our lives requires us to be both practical

that spirit over the past days makes me feel that these people are my heroes, clarify our vision and then take action to bring our dreams to life. Once we have operated from this position, it is also essential that we hold our goals with a "loose grip" and move to a place of acceptance such that you know that even if what you wanted does not happen exactly the way you wanted it to, all is for the best. I truly feel that there is an incredible coherence to our lives that we often miss and we try to control outcomes. But if we do our best, and things do not unfold according to our plans, trust that everything has happened for your highest good.

Nothing will change in your world until you assume the personal responsibility required to change. The world is a mirror: we get from it not what we want but who we are. As you reach deep into yourself, explore your most authentic values, articulate what you want to make of life and then set about manifesting these outcomes (while creating extraordinary value for the people around you), your life will begin to work at levels you never could have imagined. You can change your life in a moment: the moment you make a choice, from the deepest place within you, to stop playing small with your life and walk towards your fears. You deserve to awaken your best self. You deserve a life of joy, fulfillment and abundance. You deserve to be a star.

There is nothing so unpardonable as to consent to a senseless, aimless and purposeless life.

Helen Keller

As I've written in my book "Discover Your Destiny With The Monk Who Sold His Ferrari", the world is experiencing a shift in consciousness. More people than ever are refusing to settle for anything less than personal greatness. More people than ever are opening their hearts and standing for compassion in their communities. More people than ever are devoting themselves to excellence and realizing the fullness of their potential. This is what leadership is all about. Yes, people may not understand you as you speak your truth, live with an open heart and reach for the extraordinary. Leaders, by definition, are those who stray from the crowd and do things differently. I know you are a dreamer. I

In the universe, respect the highest power, namely the creative force that directs and makes use of all things. In the same way, you must respect the highest power in yourself, for it is of the same creative kind. For this is what makes use of the rest of you, and directs your life.

Marcus Aureluis

know you want the best from life. And I know you want to make
a difference. For this I salute you. You are my hero.

Simone Weil

INSPIRATIONAL QUOTE 16

"How can you hesitate? Risk! Risk anything! Care no more for
the opinions of others, for those voices. Do the hardest thing on
earth for you. Act for yourself. Face the truth."

Katherine Mansfield

5 WAYS TO RUN YOUR LIFE LIKE AN ELITE PERFORMER

⊙

1. Make a personal commitment to add more value than you are
paid.

2. Live out of your imagination rather than out of your memory
by constantly envisioning yourself having all you want.

3. Get in the habit of blessing your money and silently hoping
that it helps the person you give it to.

4. Spend one hour this week journalling about your beliefs around
money life that keep you in simple practices that I share with them and
resistance to having more.

5. Carve our 90 minutes every Sunday morning or night to
envision, create and then plan the week that is about to unfold.
First mentally engage with this picture of your best week by
imagining it (with color and as much emotion as possible). See
yourself performing at your highest level at work and at home.
Feel yourself having fun and making great choices in every
moment of every day. Then record this vision in your journal,

THE MASTERY MANUAL

with detail and in a committed way. Articulate not only your work intentions but also what you are dedicated to doing (and being) and home and with self. Once this is done, meticulously plan out the next 7 days in your day planner/on your tablet.

2. Discipline yourself to get up an hour earlier every morning. Most of us sleep far more than we need to. Life slips away while we are slumbering under with sheets. Yes, proper sleep is essential for elite performance and a healthy life. But excess sleep robs you of the chance to claim your destiny.

3. Focus on your best and delegate the rest. We all have certain activities which, when we do them, create our best weeks. For me the content for my books, coaching and speeches, time spent with my team having conversations around our vision and reading so that I stay sharp and focused. In your journal, start to engage in a written conversation with self around what things you should be doing most of the time to create the greatest results. Then delegate or stop doing all those time wasting, low leverage things that suck the life out of your days and dreams.

4. Every morning, celebrate 3 wins from the previous day. This is a powerful discipline to help you keep your momentum and energy high. Write down 3 things from the day before that helped you play your best game. They might be exercising, making the

QUESTIONS TO JOURNAL ON

1. What would (insert your name) look like if you were operating in your most authentic form and living the highest version of your highest vision?

2. What has been the value of your most painful experiences and how would your life be less if you had not had the benefit of them?

3. What would you be willing to die for?

4. What lessons are you most resisting in your life right now?

5. Who on the planet is living the life you dream of living and what is it about their life that speaks to you so deeply?

big sales call, taking the time to connect with your life's mission or being kind in a challenging moment. Connecting with your wins at the front end of your day sets you up for success.

5. Constantly ask yourself these 2 questions: 'is what I am doing in this moment the best use of my time?' and 'is this activity getting me closer to my goals or drawing me away from them?'

4

WORK AS A PLANET CLASS PERFORMANCE

INSPIRATIONAL QUOTES

"The path to excellence is to halt – NOW! – all un-excellent stuff."

Tom Peters

I RECENTLY HAD the good fortune to watch U2's Concert Live at Slane Castle on DVD. It was an unforgettable experience. I was inspired by Bono's passion. I was inspired by U2's devotion to excellence when it comes to working as a team and delivering an experience that is rare. And I was moved by the authentic commitment of each of the group members to play their hearts out and create value for the fans that had the privilege to be at the concert.

Marcus Aurelius

"When was the last time you had a real conversation with one of your co-workers, not about the weather or about your favorite sports team but about your lives?"

Tom Chappell
Founder of Tom's of Maine

Viewing Live at Slane Castle made me think about U2 as a high-performance team. The way they operated over those few hours can offer many lessons for you as you seek to play your biggest game not only professionally but personally. I invite you to make the time to watch the concert and to reflect on what gifts these

you have failed to give them something to be passionate about.
Assume total responsibility. Understand that great leadership
is ... Understand that watching is all about change. The world is run
under a series of timeless and immutable natural laws. Align your ...

INSPIRATIONAL QUOTES

"It is not because things are difficult that we do not dare. It is
because we do not dare that things are difficult."

Seneca

Pappa Wallenda
The Great High Wire Walker

"You can accomplish anything in
life, provided that you do not mind who gets the credit."

Harry S. Truman

QUESTIONS TO JOURNAL ON

1. If you had only five minutes left to live, who would you call
and what would you say?

2. If you could have dinner with 5 people on the planet today,

help? Could they help and why would you want to connect with them?

3. What one thing could you do that if you did it on a daily basis, your life would rise to its next level?

4. Of all your relationships, which one would benefit by you being more caring, compassionate and thoughtful?

5. What daily act could you do to make the world a better place?

5 Ways to Beat the Stress Habit

1. Ask yourself: "will this crisis really matter one year from now?

2. Press the pause button on your life for 5 minutes and go for a walk in fresh air

3. Drink more water (science confirms that drinking more water improves brain function)

4. Pour out what is worrying you into your journal. The very act of letting go onto paper will help you release the worries' hold on you.

5. Express how you are feeling to a trusted colleague

...opportunities ...ment. Even the most painful changes we can experience such as divorce, accidents, illness or death offer us powerful lessons. As human beings we have a choice. We can resist the change and crumble or we can accept the change, experience the feelings they provoke and then consciously respond with the true light of our power.

6. Remember that it's risky out on the limbs but, in this world, that's where all the fruit is. On your deathbed, what will fill your heart with the greatest regret will not be all the risks you've taken. What will fill you with the greatest sadness in your final moments will be all the risks you failed to take, all the opportunities you did not seize and all the things you did not do. People are happiest when they are growing and living their lives out on the skinny branch. Actually we are most alive when we are confronting our fears, dealing with challenges and responding to the unexpected. Why resist these "growth/life opportunities" when deep within you know that they are the stepping stones to your most authentic life?

INSPIRATIONAL QUOTES

"Real love begins where nothing is expected in return."

Antoine De Saint-Exupery

"In about the same degree as you are helpful, you will be happy."

Karl Reiland

"The more value you create for others, the more your life will work. Commit yourself to doing good. To get more from life, you must give more to life."

Robin Sharma

MY PERSONAL PRACTICES FOR HIGH-ENERGY AND PEAK HEALTH

QUESTIONS TO JOURNAL ON

1. If there was one word I would want my life to stand for, what would that one word be?

As you move through your days to create your best year yet, it is essential that you have the energy, vitality and good health to play

2. What will I no longer tolerate in my life?

your highest game. Here are some of the rituals I generally follow

3. If there was one thing I could change in my life to lift it to its

to keep healthy.

highest level, what would that one thing be?

1. Do not eat after 7 pm.

4. What has been the biggest turning point of my life and

2. Drink plenty of water throughout the day.

how has it served me by helping me become the person that

3. Drink freshly squeezed fruit juice daily.

I currently am?

4. Take daily vitamins and minerals.

5. If I had 30 days left to live, what would I do?

5. Eat less.

6. Exercise 4-5 times a week (weight and cardio).

7. Hire a personal trainer (money well spent).

17
5

THE MAKE YOUR MARK QUESTION
THE STEVE JOBS QUESTION

I'VE BEEN THINKING a lot about the Late Apple CEO Steve Jobs lately — his winning ways with the iPod, his transformation of Apple, his achievements with film studio Pixar. He was a pretty interesting guy, from what I can gather. Brilliant. Driven. Passionate. He was also a philosopher. Jobs spent some formative time in India. He studied with sages. He visited meditation retreats. He pondered life's big questions. Speaking of questions, I've heard there's one in particular that he asked himself every time he faced a big decision or choice point in his life: "...what would I do if this was the last night of my life?" I love it.

No one on their death bed ever regretted the risks that they took. What will be the least security is in the security zone. To live a big

I HAVE A confession to make: for some reason I've been reading obituaries on a regular basis these days. Not sure why I guess I like... You might think that connecting to the fact that one day you will die is a depressing thing to consider. To me it's just the opposite — connecting to my mortality breathes more life into my days. It energizes me. What I want to encourage you to consider, more than anything

the generations who will follow you that you have walked the
planet? What will be your mark? Steve Jobs met his wife that
way. He was giving a speech at a university and spotted her in
the audience. He met her after the event and wanted to take her
to dinner – but he had a business meeting. As he walked to his
car, he asked himself: "if this was the last night of my life, what
would I do?" He ran back to the auditorium and found her. They
were together since.

I read obituaries to teach me more about what a well-lived life
looks like. I learn what to do from the good ones and what to
avoid from the not so great ones. Too many people don't really
get what life's all about until they are just about to die. I don't
want to be one of them. And my guess is neither do you.

This is a great time to reflect. You are leaving one year and
welcoming in another. Go deep. Reflect on what To Dos you
have not done because fear got in the way. Think about how
quickly life is passing and what needs to get done so you feel you
played your best game as a human being. And then walk out into
the world and do it.

INSPIRATIONAL QUOTES

"Games are the most elevated forms of investigation."

Albert Einstein

"The key to success is to keep thinking unconventional thoughts."

Trevor Baylis

INSPIRATIONAL QUOTES

"Risks, I like to say, always pay off. You learn what to do or
what not to do."

Malcolm Bricklin

"The things that most people see as failures are the steps
to success."

Jonas Salk

"Success doesn't just occur. It takes effort and sacrifice.
Extraordinary people are simply those willing to do the things
ordinary people are not willing to do."

Robin Sharma

"I know that if I failed I wouldn't regret that but I knew the one
thing I might regret is not trying."

Jeff Bezos, founder of Amazon.com

"The person who tries to do everything achieves nothing."

HARVEY KEITEL AND WINDOWS OF OPPORTUNITY Robin Sharma

I don't always get it right. Please know I try so hard to walk my talk and to ensure my video is in alignment with my audio. But I'm a human being, and that means I sometimes flip. Here's what I mean.

YOUR 4 MINUTE MILE

LEADING THROUGH FEARLESSNESS

The philosopher Arthur Schopenhauer once observed: "most people take the limits of their vision to be the limits of the world. A few do not. Join them." Profound point. The life you see this very moment isn't necessarily the life of your future. You might be viewing things through the eyes of your fears, limitations and false assumptions. Once you clean up the stained glass window you see the world through, guess what? A whole new set of possibilities appear. Remember, we see the world not as it is but as we are. That idea changed my life.

I spend a lot of time encouraging the readers of my books and the participants at my workshops to "run toward your fears" and to seize those "cubic centimeters of chance" (opportunities) when they present themselves. I challenge clients to dream, to shine and to dare, because to me a life well-lived is all about reaching for your highest and best. And most of the time, I am a poster boy for visiting the places that scare me and doing the very things that make me feel uncomfortable. But recently, I didn't. Sorry.

THIS MODULE IS dedicated to inspiring you to become a genuine leader in your life by showing up as fearless in every thing that you do. Perhaps, the best way to lift your life to its highest level is to pay attention to the fears that keep you small and then to methodically take action in transcending them. For me, my fears represent huge opportunities for growth and transformation. The more I walk towards my fears, the quicker I move toward my freedom. And so my challenge to you is simply this: walk towards the places that scare you and move into the possibilities of your life (because this is where the possibility lives).

I was downtown at The Four Seasons in Toronto, in the lobby getting ready for a speech I was about to give to a company called Advanced Medical Optics that is a long-standing coaching client of ours and an impressive organization. I look up and guess who I see? Harvey Keitel. Yes, the Harvey "Reservoir Dogs Big Movie Star" Keitel. And what does the man who wrote The Monk do? I shrink from greatness.

The 4-minute mile barrier. But after Roger Bannister broke it many more replicated his feat within weeks. Why? Because he showed people what was possible. And then armed with that belief, people did the impossible.

What's your "4-minute mile"? What bill of goods have you sold yourself as to what's impossible? What false assumptions are you making in terms of what you cannot have, do and be? Your thinking creates your reality. If you think something cannot occur

I don't know why I didn't stand up and walk over and make a new friend. I've done it with baseball legend Pete Rose at the Chicago airport (we ended up sitting next to each other all the

THE MASTERY MANUAL

way to Phoenix). I did it last month with Henry Kravis, one of the planet's top financiers in the lobby of a hotel in Rome (I was with my kids and Colby thought he was cool). I did it with Senator Edward Kennedy when I saw him in Boston. I even did it with guitar virtuoso Eddie Van Halen when I was a kid growing up in Halifax, Nova Scotia. But I missed the chance to connect with Harvey Keitel.

AMBIDEXTROUS LEADERSHIP

Each day, life will send you little windows of opportunity.

I gave 2 speeches for IBM India in Mumbai earlier this month. While I was there, I had a cup of coffee with one of their executives. Like Steve Jobs, he too was a philosopher, only dressed in business clothing. In our far-reaching conversation, he made many points that I found fascinating. One in particular has really got me thinking. "Ambidextrous leadership is the key to success and fulfillment," he said. "It's all yin and yang." Here's what I think he meant: the key to greatness lies in a single word: balance. It's all balance. Balance work with family. Balance doing with thinking. Balance head with heart. Balance being friendly with being firm. Balance compassion with courage. Balance making it happen with letting it happen. And balance freedom and being spontaneous with being responsible. Life and leadership is full of paradoxes. The only way I know of to resolve them is to strike that beautiful balance. Is it easy? No. Is it worth it? Absolutely.

I CHALLENGE YOU TO PLAY YOUR BIGGEST GAME

SMALL DAILY ACTS OF YOUR GREATNESS (SDAG)

HUMAN BEINGS WERE designed to be challenged. The challenges in our professional as well as our personal lives tend to draw the greatness out of us and shake us out of our complacency. Challenge causes us to stretch and to let go of control. Challenge helps us discover our greatest gifts, highest capacities and our authentic selves.

A LIFE OF greatness is not reserved for the chosen few: women and men with perfect skin, flawless teeth and a royal pedigree. There are no extra human beings on the planet and every single one of us, I deeply believe, can choose to create a life of greatness and extraordinary meaning. It all comes down to Small Daily Acts of Greatness (SDAG). I have been teaching this principle frequently at The Elite Performers Series leadership workshop as well as at the Awakening Best Self Weekend (ABS) and the impact has been profound. Essentially, a great life is nothing more than a series of great, well-lived days strung together like a necklace of pearls. As you live your days, so you create your life. The point really is: if you show up fully each and every day and play your best game during the waking hours of

Over the next 30 days, I gently offer you the following challenges:

- I challenge you to be a dreamer in a world where all too many people have given up on standing for their dreams.
- I challenge you to be the most positive person you know, in a world where negativity prevails and cynicism is considered cool.
- I challenge you to do 3 things that you are afraid to do (because

- I challenge you to exercise regularly, eat impeccably and treat your body as a temple. Out the picture screen of your imagination, rehearse the perfect outcome.

- I challenge you to be a better mate, a more loving parent and a more contributing member. The more you can read and learn about the areas which cause you to be fearful, the more powerful you will grow.

- I challenge you to spend 60 minutes every morning in a "Holy Hour", reflecting on what you want your life to stand for and reading from something deep and inspiring.

- I challenge you to devote yourself to excellence in a society where too many people accept mediocrity.

- I challenge you to be a light on a planet filled with too much darkness; and to do good deeds daily — even if they go unrecognized.

...base a little bit more. Be more loving. Be more innovative. Take more risks. Develop deeper relationships. And dream even 1%.

...your great days will lead you to your great life.

"The smallest of actions is always better than the noblest of intentions".

Robin Sharma, "Who Will Cry When You Die?"

Inspirational Quotes

"You can preach a better sermon with your life than with your lips."

Oliver Goldsmith

"If you confront your problems rather than avoid them, you will be in a better position to deal with them."

His Holiness The Dalai Lama

"Ideation without execution is nothing more than delusion."

Robin Sharma

Questions to Journal On

1. If the five people you spend most of your time with were asked how they would describe you as a human being, what would they say?

2. If your tombstone could only have one line on it, what would that line say?

3. What has been the single most important turning point in your life and what are the five primary lessons that you learned from it?

4. How would you rate the quality of your life, at this very moment, on a scale of 1 to 10 (10 being extraordinary)? What made you come up with this number?

5 BEST PRACTICES TO LIVE YOUR BEST LIFE

1. Get up at 5:00 a.m. every morning and take 60 minutes to work on yourself.

2. Surround yourself with people who are living the life you want to live.

3. Be the kindest person you know.

4. Read from the wisdom literature for at least 30 minutes every day.

5. Run towards your fears and do what you are afraid to do.

7

BE A LIFE LONG LEARNER

⊙

CARRY A BOOK wherever you go. We spend so much time waiting in line, sitting in traffic and waiting on appointments. Why not use that time for stretching your mind, reading great literature or listening to powerful CDs? Most people feel that they do not have the time to read, but with a little creativity, you can find the time.

1. Take a speed-reading course. Reading is a powerful way to gain many years of experience from a few hours of study. For example, most biographies reflect the strategies and philosophies of great leaders or courageous individuals. Read them and model them. Speed reading will allow you to digest large quantities of material in relatively small periods of time.

2. Some top performers read a book in a day. Seek out

knowledge and information. We have truly entered the age of massive information and those who are proactive can use this to their advantage. The more you know, the less you fear.

3. All the answers to any questions are in print. How to improve as a public speaker, how to improve your relations with others, how to become fitter or develop a better memory – all aspects of personal development are dealt with in books. Therefore, in order to achieve your maximum potential, you must read daily.

4. Books help you to see what is already in yourself. That is what enlightenment is all about.

5. Read more, learn more, laugh more and love more.

6. Remember The Principle of Association: "who you will be 5 years from today essentially comes down to 2 primary influences: the people you spend your days with and the books you read."

INSPIRATIONAL QUOTES

"Life is short. Do not forget about the most important things in our life, living for other people and doing good for them."

Marcus Aurelius

"When a person dies, he leaves his belongings at home, his family at the graveside and the only thing that accompanies him are his deeds."

Eastern Saying

"Fix your course to a star and you can navigate any storm."

Da Vinci

"The books that help you the most are those that make you think the most. The hardest way of learning is that of easy reading: but a great book that comes from a great thinker is a ship of thought, deep freighted with truth and beauty."

Theodore Parker

QUESTIONS TO JOURNAL ON

The end of the summer season brings with it a wonderful opportunity to reflect on the way you are conducting both your professional and your personal life and to make those all important course corrections that will lift you to the next level of living. I find, in my own life, that if I carve out a few hours every week to engage in a little self-reflection within the pages of my journal, my priorities become clearer and new opportunities for growth and self-improvement seem to present themselves.

As I mention in my books, one of my personal practices involves the use of asking myself pointed questions that encourage me to go deep and think about the things that truly count for me. Here are some of the questions I use that I believe will help you:

1. What would the child you once were think of the adult you have become?

2. How old would you be if you did not know how old you were?

3. What 3 things could you do over the next 30 days to raise your life to its next level of excellence and festivity (and what is preventing you from doing them)?

4. What do you want your life to look like, in every area (career, personal, spiritual) 24 months from now?

5. What 5 things make you happiest in your life?

THE 11 RULES FOR A DEEPLY REWARDING LIFE

1. Place people over possessions.

2. Never stop doing what you love.

3. Always stay true to yourself.

4. Remember that we see the world not as it is but as we are.

5. Turn your wounds into wisdom and look for the gifts of your failures.

6. Be the kindest person you know.

7. Do at least one thing every day that makes your palms sweat.

8. Read from the wisdom literature for at least 30 minutes each day.

9. Spend at least one hour a week in silence and nature to renew yourself.

10. Commit to a serious exercise program to awaken your best physical life.

11. Dedicate yourself to making your mark and leaving a legacy.

8

Destiny and Leadership

⊙

As I wrote in "The Saint, The Surfer & The CEO": "there are no extra people on the planet." By this I mean that every single one of us is here for a reason and a specific mission. Like the famed psychologist Abraham Maslow, I genuinely believe that each human being has embedded into their genetic makeup a calling and a cause. For some, this calling may be manifested as running a country, a company or a community. For others, it may be raising a family of leaders or showing leadership through their art, poetry or public service. Each and every one of us has a destiny and our life begins to work at its highest level when our days become an expression of that central mission.

At my seminars, so many people ask me: "Robin, how do I discover my destiny?" My response is always the same: "you

cannot discover your destiny – your destiny will discover you."
The best move you can make is to do the inner work required
to come to know yourself at the deepest level. Journal, meditate
and perform patient reflection so that you come to know your
most authentic values, your highest beliefs and what kind of life
you really want to create. The deeper you go, the more you will
know. And the more you will know, the easier it will be to spot
the signs that will lead you to your destiny. Once you find it, your
best game as a human being will begin to unfold.

INSPIRATIONAL QUOTES

"And what is as important as knowledge?" asked the mind.
"Caring and seeing with the heart," answered the soul."

Flavia

"We are not human if we can no longer experience awe and
wonder at the beauty and mystery of life."

Charlene Spretnak

"Business is not first and foremost about making money or
products or offering services. Business, as commerce, is above all
a vehicle for achieving personal and organizational greatness. It is
for accomplishing something worthy and noble."

Peter Koestenbaum

How to Live a Big Life

I invite you to begin to reflect on what your life would look like at its highest most spectacular level. The more you can have conversations (with other people and with yourself through the power of journaling) around what it is you want to create as you experience life, the more conviction you will bring to making this happen. In your days, do you take actions and advance intentions that reflect the highest possibilities of who you are? Or do your days act on you and pass quickly without you bringing your creativity to your moments? A great standard to set for yourself is to commit to your life representing what's possible as a human being. Here are 5 philosophies that will help you:

1. Record a Definite Chief Aim statement. This is a one paragraph summary of what you want your life to stand for. Read it 3 times a day (morning, noon and night). Also verbalize it as much as possible to deepen the commitment that you bring to it.

2. Create a dream team for yourself. Find people whose lives are working and who are living the kind of life that you want to create. Have lunch with them on a regular basis. Call them from time to time and engage with them at a deep level of conversation. Their ideas and personal habits will influence you and help you step into the possibilities that your life presents to you.

3. Create success structures. Every great life is built on a

foundation of structures that support its success. Examples of success structures that you might want to build into your weeks include working with a personal trainer a few times a week, a weekly – mastermind meeting, engaging a life coach, taking vitamins and supplements every day, a specific period each week for planning and visioning and a regular nature walk.

4. Take big action. There is a fine balance between making things happen and letting things happen. Life is always a balance between doing and being. A wise leader strikes the ideal balance. There is no replacement for good old hard work and taking "big action" to create the experience of life you want. There is an old saying that says "heaven helps those who help themselves." Each day, do something that will stretch you and advance the mission that is your life.

5. Pay attention to your associations. If you want to know what your life will look like 5 years from now, reflect on the 10 people you spend most of your time with. The orbit that you live within (in terms of the people you spend your time with), will define the kind of person you will become and the kind of life you will lead. Play your highest game, surround yourself with people and have conversations with individuals who are committed to greatness, leadership and personal responsibility.

9

The Power of Your Associations

⊙

There's a line that I have been sharing with audiences at my presentations and workshops these days and it can be simply stated: "you are who you have lunch with." As you enter into what I hope will be your best year yet, take a few moments to reflect on the fact that you become who you associate with. You will take on the thinking, philosophies and even the behaviors of the people who you spend most of your time with. Often, this process occurs at an unconscious level and we don't even know we are being influenced by those around us. Trust that there is great power in association and we do become deeply affected by the company we keep.

Are you spending time with people who are living the kind of life you dream of living? Are you having conversations with your heroes? Do your friends and associates uplift you and inspire you to stand for something greater than you currently are? Or do they bring you down and frustrate you – limiting you and your possibilities? And remember: your associations not only come in human forms. I do believe that we become the books we read because reading is nothing more than having a conversation with the author. When we read books written by the greatest among us, the highest place within us can be stirred and the ideas that we learn can compel us to take the new action that creates better results. The big idea: as we learn more, we can do more. And as we know better, we can choose better.

We are at the beginning of a new year. I gently challenge you to record at least 10 of the lessons you learned from the year that has passed onto a piece of paper. Then, articulate, not only the goals that are important for you to achieve in this year, but the philosophy you want to live your professional as well as your personal life by over the coming months. Setting your intentions down onto paper sets into play powerful causes that will yield wonderful effects. And as you do this reflection and goal-setting exercise, think about your associations. Think about the people you choose to surround yourself with. Think about your environmental influences and what you are allowing into the precious palace of your mind. I know you know this: what goes on inside determines what goes on on the outside. Your thinking does form your world. And we can only act on the ideas that are in our minds. When we know better, we truly can do better. With better awareness you can make better choices.

Inspirational Quotes

"Thoughts which are mixed with any of the feelings of emotions constitute a "magnetic" force which attracts other similar or related thoughts."

Napoleon Hill

"If you confront your problems rather than avoid them, you will be in a better position to deal with them."

His Holiness The Dalai Lama

"When you think about it, we are really not here that long. Speak to someone in their 80's or 90's and they will reflect on the fact that they cannot believe how quickly life passed. Time slips through our fingers like grains of sand, never to return again. Today, live boldly, with passion, excellence and love. Run towards the things that frighten you. Champion those around you. And dig deeper to allow more of who you truly are to see the light of day."

Robin Sharma

8 WAYS TO RESTORE BALANCE IN YOUR LIFE

1. Take a 60 minute Holy Hour at the beginning of each day and nourish your mind, body, emotions and spirit.

2. Spend some time in nature on a weekly basis.

3. Write "love letters" to those who need to be appreciated.

4. Experience silence, solitude and stillness for at least 10 minutes each day.

5. Do the things that made you happy as a kid.

6. Get serious about exercise because nothing is more important than your health.

7. Write in a journal to promote clarity of thought and deepen your insight.

8. Find a cause larger than yourself and give back to others.

QUESTIONS TO JOURNAL ON

1. What are the three biggest barriers keeping you from creating the life you want?

2. What are the 3 main things that drain your energy and keep you from living your best life?

3. What are 3 risks you need to take that you have been resisting?

4. What are the 5 most important things you learned from last year?

5. What 5 words will stand for what you want to make of your life?

THE VALUE OF "MICROADVENTURES"

So many of the participants who attend the Awakening Best Self Weekend (ABS) 2-day personal transformation workshop, come to the event in search of practical tools that will help them find sustained happiness. One of the ideas I have been teaching recently is the concept of what I call "microadventures". When we were kids, much of our happiness came from the fact that we did so many of the things we loved to do. We would skip stones on a lake or make angels in the snow or simply playfully engage in the present moment. Often, as we age, we stop doing the things that made us so happy in our youth. We give up that musical instrument that made our soul sing. Or we stopped playing hockey or going skiing or surfing. Or we stopped spending quality time with the friends that used to make us laugh so hard we thought our bellies would burst. To make big transformations, the key is to take small daily steps. The journey of 1,000 miles truly does begin with a single step and by engaging in "microadventures", little adventures that you inject into your weeks - you will restore the passion that you may have lost.

Taking an hour over the weekend to go to your favorite bookstore and browse through your favorite section, might be a microadventure you can engage in next week. Or trying Vietnamese food if you have never tasted it before, it would be another microadventure. Or going for snowboarding lessons, picking up the phone and having a conversation with someone you admire, or going hiking in the woods could be other microadventures that you could schedule into your weeks, bringing greater happiness and fulfillment in your days. Remember, the things that get scheduled are the things that get done and scheduling at least one microadventure into your week will do wonders for the way that you think, feel and act.

10

A Salute to My Heroes

⊙

I've just come off a weekend spent with a band of dreamers.
The latest Awakening Best Self Weekend (ABS) drew people
from Mexico, Puerto Rico, The United States and Canada – an
extraordinary group of courageous souls dedicated to playing
their highest games as human beings. On Friday night, CEOs,
homemakers, students, entrepreneurs, artists and teachers
walked in wearing their usual social masks and wondering
what was about to occur over the weekend process. By Sunday
afternoon, stunning transformations had taken place as people had
transcended their largest fears, confronted their resistance's and
made heartfelt commitments to shining at their brightest as they
walked out into the world. The level of love in that conference
room was incredible. And, the courage that I observed in

that room over the 2 $^{1/2}$ days makes me feel that these people are my heroes.

Nothing will change in your world until you assume the personal responsibility required to change. The world is a mirror: we get from it not what we want but who we are. As you reach deep into yourself, explore your most authentic values, articulate what you want to make of life and then set about manifesting these outcomes (while creating extraordinary value for the people around you), your life will begin to work at levels you never could have imagined. You can change your life in a moment: the moment you make a choice, from the deepest place within you, to stop playing small with your life and walk towards your fears. You deserve to awaken your best self. You deserve a life of joy, fulfillment and abundance. You deserve to be a star.

As I've written in my book "Discover Your Destiny With The Monk Who Sold His Ferrari", the world is experiencing a shift in consciousness. More people than ever are refusing to settle for anything less than personal greatness. More people than ever are opening their hearts and standing for compassion in their communities. More people than ever are devoting themselves to excellence and realizing the fullness of their potential. This is what leadership is all about. Yes, people may not understand you as you speak your truth, live with an open heart and reach for the extraordinary. Leaders, by definition, are those who stray from the crowd and do things differently. I know you are a dreamer. I know you want the best from life. And I know you want to make a difference. For this I salute you. You are my hero.

Inspirational Quotes

"How can you hesitate? Risk! Risk anything! Care no more for the opinions of others, for those voices. Do the hardest thing on earth for you. Act for yourself. Face the truth."

Katherine Mansfield

"A dreamer is one who can only find his way by moonlight, and his punishment is that he sees the dawn before the rest of the world."

Oscar Wilde

"You have a duty to shine and if you refuse to accept this responsibility, the world will be a lesser place as a result of this retreat in courage."

Robin Sharma

QUESTIONS TO JOURNAL ON

1. What is the best book you've ever read and why?

2. What are your 3 largest fears and how have they limited you over the years of your life?

3. What do you want your life to stand for?

4. On a piece of paper, list the 10 organizing principles that you commit to living the rest of your life by.

11

Leadership Lesson of the Month

⊙

The following paragraph is an excerpt from my book "Leadership Wisdom from The Monk Who Sold His Ferrari: The 8 Rituals of Visionary Leaders". In this segment of the story, the main character Julian Mantle is sharing his leadership philosophy with his former golf partner, an entrepreneur who is now struggling with a changing business culture. At page 65 of the book, Julian states as follows:

"Stop blaming your people for your leadership failures. Stop blaming the changing economy, increased regulation and competitive pressures. If people haven't bought into your vision, it's because they haven't bought into your leadership. If they are not loyal, it's because you have not given them enough reasons to be loyal. If they are not passionate about their work, it's because you have failed to give them something to be passionate about. Assume total responsibility. Understand that great leadership precedes great followership."

INSPIRATIONAL QUOTES

"It is not because things are difficult that we do not dare. It is because we do not dare that things are difficult."

Seneca

"Life is lived out on the wire. The rest is just waiting."

Pappa Wallenda

The Great High Wire Walker "You can accomplish anything in life, provided that you do not mind who gets the credit."

Harry S. Truman

QUESTIONS TO JOURNAL ON

1. If you had only five minutes left to live, who would you call and what would you say?

2. If you could have dinner with 5 people on the planet today,

who would they be and why would you want to connect with them?

3. What one thing could you do that if you did it on a daily basis, your life would rise to its next level?

4. Of all your relationships, which one would benefit by you being more caring, compassionate and thoughtful?

5. What daily act could you do to make the world a better place?

5 WAYS TO BEAT THE STRESS HABIT

1. Ask yourself: "will this crisis really matter one year from now?"

2. Press the pause button on your life for 5 minutes and go for a walk in fresh air

3. Drink more water (science confirms that drinking more water improves brain function)

4. Pour out what is worrying you into your journal. The very act of letting go onto paper will help you release the worries' hold on you.

5. Express how you are feeling to a trusted colleague

PERSONAL LEADERSHIP THROUGH ANGER
MASTERY

The following story is helpful in times of frustration:

There was once a young boy who often was angry. His father decided to give him a bag of nails one afternoon saying: "son, when you get angry take one of these nails and simply nail it into the fence in our backyard. You will feel better by releasing your frustration." After the first day, the young boy had nailed 25 nails into the fence.

But as the weeks went by, the young boy grew more aware of his anger and put fewer and fewer nails into the fence. Although he never denied the anger that was there, in time, he found it easier to silently experience his anger and then release it rather than angrily nail the nails into the fence.

Finally, the day came when the young boy stopped losing his temper completely. On that day, his father said to him: "son, now go to that fence and pull out a nail for each day that you did not manage your anger and hold it in a responsible way. A day later, the boy went to his father and told him that each nail had been removed from the fence. The father replied: "I am proud of you son. I would like you to look at the holes that you have made in the fence. When things are said in anger, irritation or frustration, you can put a hole into someone just like you have put a hole into that fence. Although you may retract your words and apologize, the scar can remain for a long, long time. So be kind. Be compassionate. And care for all the people in your life. Life is a short journey and relationships are most important."

As you go through your workweek, reflect on the people that you work with and ask yourself whether you are showing up at your best with them and treating them as the magnificent people that they truly are.

12

LEADERSHIP THROUGH
FEARLESSNESS

⊙

THIS MODULE IS dedicated to inspiring you to become
a genuine leader in your life by showing up as fearless in every
thing that you do. Perhaps, the best way to lift your life to its
highest level is to pay attention to the fears that keep you small
and then to methodically take action in transcending them.
For me, my fears represent huge opportunities for growth and
transformation. The more I walk towards my fears, the quicker
I move toward my freedom. And so my challenge to you is
simply this: walk towards the places that scare you and move
into the unknown spaces of your life (because this is where
the possibility lives).

INSPIRATIONAL QUOTES

"Where you stumble there your treasure lies."

Joseph Campbell

"To venture causes anxiety, but not to venture is to lose one's self... and to venture in the highest is precisely to be conscious of one's self."

Kierkegaard

"Leadership is not about managing things but about developing people. Visionary leaders are those who understand that the true assets of any organization go up the elevator in the morning and down it every night."

Robin Sharma

"Learning is remembering."

Socrates

"Read the best books first, otherwise you'll find you do not have time."

Henry David Thoreau

"The scholar who thinks but does not create is like the cloud which does not give rain."

Eastern Wisdom

Self Leadership Through Fearlessness: 5 Practices

1. Have conversations about the things that you fear. Business is nothing more than a conversation: lose the conversations with your clients and teammates and eventually you will lose the business. The more conversations you can have around the things that you fear, the more the death of your fears will be certain. Putting a voice to the things that keep you small in your life allows you to bring them into the light of awareness where they dissolve (just like shadows always dissolve in the light of the day).

2. Feel your fears. So often in our society, we are encouraged to disregard our fears and to simply "think positive thoughts". This is nothing more than engaging in denial which is not only ineffective, it is unhealthy. When a fear surfaces for you, whether it is the fear of giving a big presentation or calling a big prospect, acknowledge your fears. Befriend your fears. Notice where they live in terms of the sensations within your body (often fear appears as a knot in the stomach). By paying attention to your fears, they will lose their hold on you.

3. Practice. The more prepared you are, the less limiting your fears will be. If you are afraid of asking for the sale or dealing with a difficult employee, engage in mental rehearsal and visualization. On the picture screen of your imagination, rehearse the perfect outcome.

4. Education. The more you can read and learn about the areas which cause you to be fearful, the more powerful you will grow. If you are afraid of taking your business to the next level because you feel it will become overly complex and stressful, for example, read the biographies of people who have walked the path before you. Step into their mindsets and see how they did what they did.

5. Create a chant. Affirmations are highly effective tools to help you program and re-script your beliefs. Create a simple one or two line "chant" that you can repeat frequently through your day to keep you at your highest game and within your most powerful state. Your chant might look something like this: "I am an elite performer seeing change as opportunity and having fun while I create success."

Great Leadership at Work: 6 Traits

Here are 6 traits of authentic leaders who are change evangelists within their workplaces:

1. They are discreetly vulnerable. In other words, they wear their heart on their sleeves but do so with good judgment.

2. They are relentlessly inventive. In other words, they constantly seek new solutions to old problems.

3. They are tightly focused. In other words, they realize that time is the most precious commodity of life.

4. They are value driven. In other words, they realize that money is a byproduct of adding deep value to all stakeholders.

5. They are shamelessly passionate. In other words, they realize that passion is contagious and are models of enthusiasm.

6. They are community centered. In other words, they realize that at the end of the day, nothing is more important in business and in life than relationships.

QUESTIONS TO JOURNAL ON

1. What are you most resisting in your life at this moment?

2. What will you no longer tolerate in your life?

3. What one thing could you do on a regular basis to lift your life to its highest level?

13

THE MANY FORMS OF WEALTH

⊙

WHAT IS WEALTH? In my mind, there are many forms of wealth. Most people consider wealth to be a purely economic commodity. But to me, there are five forms of wealth: economic wealth, relationship wealth, physical wealth, adventure wealth and what I call psychic wealth (which is all about filling your life with meaning). If one doesn't attend to each of these, I believe they will live a hollow life.

Economic wealth is obvious. Money is important to live your best life. It takes money to travel or to pay for your children's tennis lessons or to pay for university. But that's just one form of wealth. If all an individual has is economic wealth, I believe that they still lack authentic wealth. One must also have relationship wealth. This is all about feeling connected to other human beings and forging a strong and loving community around you. One must also build physical wealth – without your good health, you really have nothing. No one wants to be the richest person in the graveyard. I feel that it's also important to work on developing adventure wealth. This form of wealth is all about feeling a sense of passion within your heart and wealthy in terms of the adventures you experience as you journey through your days. Adventure wealth might be built by taking exotic trips or experiencing micro adventures such as trying a new type of food or having new conversations with an interesting person. Finally, to be authentically wealthy, each of us must create psychic wealth. The deepest need of the human heart is to live for something more important than ourselves. Lasting happiness can only come from what we give to the world and those around us as opposed to what we receive. Psychic wealth is all about living for a cause greater than yourself.

Many of us beat ourselves up because we do not have as much economic wealth as we would like to see. Money is important to live your best life. But it is not the be all and end all. Many rich people are not truly wealthy. Working on each of these five forms of wealth will inspire you to reach higher, dream bigger and to enjoy genuine fulfillment as you savor the blessing that is called your life.

INSPIRATIONAL QUOTES

"Argue for your limitations and sure enough they are yours."

Richard Bach

"When you arise in the morning, think of what a precious privilege it is to be alive – to breathe, to think, to enjoy, to love."

Marcus Aurelius

"I am surprised every morning when I wake up and I find the world intact. There is everywhere evidence of nature's optimism. The light is new, the rain is sumptuously wet. When the sun shines we know everything is possible. Every morning we are younger than we were the night before."

William Crozier

"It is not possible to make another human being feel good about themselves until you first feel good about yourself. Leadership begins within."

Robin Sharma

8 BEST TRAITS OF THE GREATEST PEOPLE

1. They are kind and relationship-centric. They put people first.

2. They are value creators and precisely focused on service. In other words, they help other people get what they want and are committed to being instruments of service.

3. They are passionate and their passion becomes contagious. They have that childlike sparkle in their eyes.

4. They are in alignment. Their video matches their audio. They are not out of integrity. They are honest, on purpose and centered.

5. They are disciplined and hard working. No great dream was ever built without hard work.

6. They are dreamers. They understand that success is all about being in the process of creating what's most important. It's a journey and they are patient.

7. They are courageous. They do what's uncomfortable and see failures as market research. They understand that failure is the price of ambition.

8. They are originals. They take the road less traveled. They think differently, they behave differently and feel differently. They see the world through a different set of eyes. And this makes them leaders.

Questions to Journal On

1. What is your least attractive trait?

2. What does a world-class life look like to you?

3. What is the best lesson that life has taught you?

14

THE POWER OF RENEWAL

⊙

AS WE GET into the warmer months, you will be presented with many opportunities to reflect on the way you are living and leading as a human being. Often, we find ourselves so busy driving we don't take the time to stop for gas. We are so busy working in our business, we don't work on our business. We are so busy acting within our careers, we don't take the time to step back and work on our careers. We are so caught up in our day to day lives, we do not press the pause button and work on our lives. And then the days slip into weeks, the weeks slip into months, the months into years and before we know it many years have past without us taking charge and creating the lives that we know in our hearts that we are meant to live. Remember, if you keep on acting the way you have always been acting, you will be certain to get the results you have always been seeing.

One of the great success tactics of the Elite Performers is that they make the time for renewal. Each day is not a game day for an elite athlete, for example they have their game days but they have their days when they renew, recharge and think about how they can get better. Work with trainers, watch tapes of past games and spend a lot of time thinking. You are an elite player not only in business but in life. Do you spend enough time being thoughtful and strategizing about the life you want to create?

Over the coming weeks, make the time to journal. Make the time to have profound conversations with people about what's most important to you. And what is not working in your life. Spend the time taking long silent walks in the woods. Go deep. Make some commitments to yourself to play your biggest game as a human being. To live life on your terms. It will be one of the best moves that you can make.

INSPIRATIONAL QUOTES

"If there is something great in you, it will not appear on your first call. It will not appear and come to you easily, without any work and effort."

Ralph Waldo Emerson

"On the other side of your fears lives your best life."

Robin Sharma

"Love provides the person with the purpose of his life. Intellect shows him the means to achieve that purpose."

Leo Tolstoy

The Death of Fear

One of the experiential exercises that has been tremendously helpful to the participants at our Awakening Best Self Weekends has been a piece we do on transforming fear into freedom. As I travel and meet people from of all walks of life around the world, I realize that the single biggest thing that prevents us from living our best lives is fear. Each of us keeps our lives much smaller than they are meant to be due to our fears. Yet, most of our fears are illusions. Most of our fears have been taught to us. Most of our living beliefs are nothing more than fantasies that we picked up along the way and made into truths. Here are five ideas to help you move through your fears:

1. What you resist will persist. As the author Sam Keen once said: "you are caught by what you are running from." Do not run away from your fears, run towards them.

2. Put a voice to your fears. Most people disown their fear and pretend that it is not there. When you speak about it, you begin to release it.

3. Write about your fears. A great way to build self awareness is to write in a journal about the things that frighten you. When you see them on paper, they have less power over you.

4. Take wise risks. Every day do something small to walk towards your fears. On the other side of every fear door there lives a precious gift.

5. Celebrate fearlessness. Every time you transcend a fear, honor yourself for your achievement.

QUESTIONS TO JOURNAL ON

1. If my life could stand for one word what would that word be?

2. How could I fill my life with a greater sense of curiosity and wonder?

3. What action am I most resisting taking in my life at this very moment?

4. As I live my days, do I curse the darkness or am I a person that lights the candle?

5. At work, do I play victim or victor?

15

CREATE A DREAM BOOK

⊙

ON A QUIET afternoon, go out and buy 10 magazines. Be sure they represent a wide variety, perhaps one with beautiful homes and lovely material things, another showing leading people and yet another with images of fit, vital and fully alive people. Then cut out the images that most appeal to you and represent your goals. Finally, paste them in a binder. Under each image write which goal this image represents, why it is important to you, what will happen to you if you do not attain it and a specific deadline for its accomplishment. This strategy has worked wonders for many of my clients.

INSPIRATIONAL QUOTES

"The opposite of love is not hate, it's indifference. And the opposite of life is not death, it's indifference."

Elie Wiesel

"No person was ever ruined from without. The final ruin comes from within."

Amelia Barr

"It's an odd world we live in. We can send a missile across the world with pinpoint accuracy yet we have trouble walking across the street to meet a new neighbor. We have no time to slow and help someone in need yet we always seem to have time to slow down to stare at the car wreck. We have trouble finding time to read to our children yet we always make time to read the valueless stories in a newspaper. Real leadership as a human being means you take some time to press the "pause button" of your life and deeply reflect on the things that truly count – and then you have the boldness to live out the rest of your life according to them. This is how anyone can live their best lives and realize their highest destiny."

Robin Sharma

How to Treat a Human Being

1. Treat every person as a unique gift. We are each as unique as our fingerprints and no one else on this planet will see the world exactly as you will. Respect, honor and cherish the differences; they are what makes us special. To make this point, I'll quote William McNamara who wrote: "I once lived near a mansion where only one of the many gardeners employed had succeeded with every one of the roses. I asked him the secret of his success. He told me that the other gardeners treated all the roses not unwisely, but too generally. They treated them all in precisely the same way; whereas he watched each rose separately and followed out for each plant its special need for soil, sun, air, water, support and shelter."

2. Speak your truth. Great leaders are vulnerable. Great leaders expose their weakness and show their humanity. Great leaders wear their hearts on their sleeves and never let an opportunity to honor another slip by without speaking from their hearts. As I say in my speeches: "before someone will lend you a hand you must touch their hearts."

3. Get behind their eyeballs. Most of the problems that surface between human beings arise from a failure to see the other person's perspective. If we could remember that one of the most important of all of the human hungers is the need to be understood and then took the time to try and see the situation from the other person's perspective, there would be far less conflict and far more harmony – both in the workplace and within the world.

4. Be polite. Peter Drucker once said: "good manners are the lubricant of an organization." To excel in business you must remember these key words that deepen relationships: "please" and "thank you". Using "please" sends the signal that you respect the recipient. Using "thank you" shows them you appreciate the receiver. Success in business is not about the big things but more about the little things. Those daily acts of kindness that connect you to the people who you have the privilege to work beside. And when you do connect to them, in a real and lasting way, the business results always speak for themselves.

HOW TO SET GOALS THAT ACHIEVE
THEMSELVES

- Write them down. As I wrote in my book "Family Wisdom from The Monk Who Sold His Ferrari": "the things that get written down are the things that get done." Writing down your goals burns them into your consciousness and heightens your awareness around them.

- Evaluate them daily. What is not measured will not be mastered. It is futile to review your goals every quarter. The key is to reflect on them daily – if even for 5 minutes. In this way, they can constantly be evaluated and you can make frequent course corrections. I rank my progress on each of my goals from 1-10 on a daily basis. This keeps me acutely aware of what I am doing right in my days and what needs to be improved.

- Share them with others. Form a Mastermind Alliance, enlisting a few of your confidants to meet every week to share your goals, discuss your strategies and share your success.

- Live from your mind's eye. Take 5 minutes every morning to vividly imprint the gorgeous vision of your future – the sum total of all your goals on the movie screen of your imagination. All things are created twice: first in your mind's eye and then in reality.

How to "Out-Innovate, Out-Perform and Out-Think" the Competition

In this new world of business we find ourselves working within, ideas are the true commodity of success. As I say in my speeches: "the greatest leaders in the new economy will be those who are dedicated to becoming the greatest thinkers." We live in a world where one idea, dreamed up inside one mind, can change the way we do things. Here are 4 simple ways you and your team can create a culture of innovation and imagination:

1. See every job as an adventure. Put on a "new set of eyes"

and see the work you do in a more lively, childlike way. Shift your mindset to see even the most mundane of tasks as an opportunity to stretch, grow and add value to your organization and its customers.

2. Reshape your environment. In my bestseller "Who Will Cry When You Die?", I suggest that we all create a pure environment, one that promotes healthy thoughts and peak performance on the playing field of life. The quality of your surroundings greatly affects the quality of your thinking. Ensure your workplace has inspiring posters and quotes in view, is uncluttered and clean and is a place where it is fun to work. Remember, the company that plays together stays together.

3. Reward "intelligent failures." I coined the term "intelligent failures" to remind us that great victories are always preceded by countless failures. Failure is the highway to success and making mistakes is the pathway to the big wins of business (and life). Rather than punishing those people on your team who take initiative but don't get it quite right the first time around, reward them for breaking out of the box and taking a beautiful risk. This will send a signal through your corporate culture: innovation matters!

4. Spend time in nature. Many readers of "The Monk Who Sold His Ferrari" have e-mailed me confirming that my suggestion of spending regular time in nature has given them million-dollar ideas that have improved both their professional and their personal lives. Communing with nature gets you away from the ringing phones and the flying faxes and connects you with the higher part of you that is intuitive, wise and imaginative. I always carry a dictaphone when I'm walking alone in the woods, because the best thoughts come to me at these times, and capturing them is crucial.

16

5 WAYS TO RUN YOUR LIFE LIKE
AN ELITE PERFORMER

⊙

I HAVE THE privilege to serve as the personal life coach to a number of high-performing CEOs and wildly successful financial traders. One of their chief requests of me sounds like this: "Robin, how can I get all I need to get done in the limited time I have, be a great partner and parent and still find some time to nurture my inner life?" Here are 5 simple practices that I share with them:

1. Carve our 90 minutes every Sunday morning or night to envision, create and then plan the week that is about to unfold. First mentally engage with this picture of your best week by imagining it (with color and as much emotion as possible). See yourself performing at your highest level at work and at home. Feel yourself having fun and making great choices in every moment of every day. Then record this vision in your journal,

with detail and in a committed way. Articulate not only your work intentions but also what you are dedicated to doing (and being) and home and with self. Once this is done, meticulously plan out the next 7 days in your day planner/on your tablet.

2. Discipline yourself to get up an hour earlier every morning. Most of us sleep far more than we need to. Life slips away while we are slumbering under with sheets. Yes, proper sleep is essential for elite performance and a healthy life. But excess sleep robs you of the chance to claim your destiny.

3. Focus on your best and delegate the rest. We all have certain activities which, when we do them, create our best weeks. For me these activities include 'face time with clients', time in solitude so I can capture creative ideas that help me develop me content for my books, coaching and speeches, time spent with my team having conversations around our vision and reading so that I stay sharp and focused. In your journal, start to engage in a written conversation with self around what things you should be doing most of the time to create the greatest results. Then delegate or stop doing all those time wasting, low leverage things that suck the life out of your days and dreams.

4. Every morning, celebrate 3 wins from the previous day. This is a powerful discipline to help you keep your momentum and energy high. Write down 3 things from the day before that helped you play your best game. They might be exercising, making the big sales call, taking the time to connect with your life's mission or being kind in a challenging moment. Connecting with your wins at the front end of your day sets you up for success.

5. Constantly ask yourself these 2 questions: 'is what I am doing in this moment the best use of my time?' and 'is this activity getting me closer to my goals or drawing me away from them?'

INSPIRATIONAL QUOTES

"The path to excellence is to halt – NOW! – all un-excellent stuff."

Tom Peters

"Stop talking about what the good person should be and just be that person."

Marcus Aurelius

"When was the last time you had a real conversation with one of your co-workers, not about the weather or about your favorite sports team but about your lives?"

Tom Chappell
Founder of Tom's of Maine

3 LESSONS FOR CHANGE MASTERY

1. Understand that Nature is all about change. The world is run under a series of timeless and immutable natural laws. Align your life with these laws and your life works. Operate against them and this resistance naturally throws your life into chaos. One of these laws is simply: nature loves change. Seasons change. The weather changes. Animals are born, they mature, they die. And so it is with our lives - they unfold as a series of changes. It is only the voice of fear within us that causes us to resist and run from change. The truth is that all change is good. It causes us to grow and evolve. And it introduces us to who we truly are. When you learn (and it is a learned skill) to love change and dance in the uncertainty of life, you open yourself up to possibility and your best days.

2. Remember that the person who experiences the most wins. When I am engaged by an organization to help them transform their employees into elite performers, the request I hear the most sounds like this: "please show them how to manage all the changes we are experiencing (as a result of a merger or the new economic landscape or the reorganization)." One of the strategies I share with the team always centers around the personal value that change brings to our lives. Change causes us to shift the way we see the world. Change, when embraced can move us out of boredom and complacency into the higher reaches of your best self. Change can help you view opportunities that previously sat dormant. Even the most painful changes we can experience such as divorce, accidents, illness or death offer us powerful lessons. As human beings we have a choice: we can resist the change and crumble or we can accept the change, experience the feelings they provoke and then consciously respond with the true light of our power.

3. Remember that it's risky out on the limb but, in this world, that's where all the fruit is. On your deathbed, what will fill your heart with the greatest regret will not be all the risks you've taken. What will fill you with the greatest sadness in your final moments will be all the risks you failed to take, all the opportunities you did not seize and all the things you did not do. People are happiest when they are growing and living their lives out on the skinny branch. Actually, we are most alive when we are confronting our fears, dealing with challenges and responding to the unexpected. Why resist these "growth/life opportunities" when deep within you know that they are the stepping stones to your most authentic life?

MY PERSONAL PRACTICES FOR HIGH-ENERGY
AND PEAK HEALTH

As you move through your days to create your best year yet, it is essential that you have the energy, vitality and good health to play your highest game. Here are some of the rituals I generally follow to keep healthy:

1. Do not eat after 7 pm.

2. Drink plenty of water throughout the day.

3. Drink freshly squeezed fruit juice daily.

4. Take vitamins and minerals daily.

5. Eat less.

6. Exercise 4-5 times a week (weight and cardio).

7. Hire a personal trainer (money well spent).

17

MAKE YOUR MARK

⊙

I HAVE A confession to make: for some reason, I've been reading obituaries on a regular basis these days. Not sure why. I guess, like most human beings, as we get to the half-time point of our lives, we connect to our mortality and realize that – no matter how long we live – our days are numbered. You might think that connecting to the fact that one day you will die is a depressing thing to consider. To me it's just the opposite – connecting to my mortality breathes more life into my days. It energizes me. It makes me want to give my best, seize every opportunity that crosses my path and stand for something higher.

What I want to encourage you to consider, more than anything else, over the next 30 days is this: "what will be your legacy?" What will be the footprint that you will leave behind to show the generations who will follow you that you have walked the planet? What will be your mark?

I read obituaries to teach me more about what a well-lived life looks like. I learn what to do from the good ones and what to avoid from the not so great ones. Too many people don't really get what life's all about until they are just about to die. I don't want to be one of them. And my guess is neither do you.

INSPIRATIONAL QUOTES

"Games are the most elevated forms of investigation."

Albert Einstein

"The key to success is to risk thinking unconventional thoughts."

Trevor Baylis

"The things that most people see as failures are the steps to success."

Malcolm Bricklin

"Success doesn't just occur. It takes effort and sacrifice. Extraordinary people are simply those willing to do the things ordinary people are not willing to do."

Robin Sharma

HARVEY KEITEL AND WINDOWS OF OPPORTUNITY

I don't always get it right. Please know I try so hard to walk my talk and to ensure my video is in alignment with my audio. But I'm a human being, and that means sometimes I slip. Here's what I mean.

I spend a lot of time encouraging the readers of my books and the participants at my workshops to "run toward your fears" and to seize those "cubic centimeters of chance" (opportunities) when they present themselves. I challenge clients to dream, to shine and to dare, because to me a life well-lived is all about reaching for your highest and best. And most of the time, I am a poster boy for visiting the places that scare me and doing the very things that make me feel uncomfortable. But recently, I didn't. Sorry.

I was downtown at The Four Seasons in Toronto, in the lobby getting ready for a speech I was about to give to a company called Advanced Medical Optics that is a long-standing coaching client of ours and an impressive organization. I look up and guess who I see? Harvey Keitel. Yes, the Harvey "Reservoir Dogs Big Movie Star" Keitel. And what does the man who wrote The Monk do? I shrink from greatness.

I don't know why I didn't stand up and walk over and make a new friend. I've done it with baseball legend Pete Rose at the Chicago airport (we ended up sitting next to each other all the way to Phoenix). I did it last month with Henry Kravis, one of the planet's top financiers in the lobby of a hotel in Rome (I was with my kids and Colby thought he was cool). I did it with Senator Edward Kennedy when I saw him in Boston. I even did it with guitar virtuoso Eddie Van Halen when I was a kid growing up in Halifax, Nova Scotia. But I missed the chance to connect with Harvey Keitel.

Each day, life will send you little windows of opportunity. Our destiny is ultimately defined by how we respond to these windows of opportunity. Shrink from them and your life will be small. Feel the fear and run to them anyway, and your life will be large. Even with your kids, you only have a little window to develop them and champion their highest potential. And to show them what unconditional love looks like. When that window closes, it never reopens.

If I see Harvey Keitel again, I promise you that I'll sprint towards him. He may think I'm a celebrity stalker until we start to chat. And then he'll discover the truth: I'm just a guy who seizes the gifts that life presents to me.

18

I Challenge You to Play Your Biggest Game

⊙

HUMAN BEINGS WERE designed to be challenged. The challenges in our professional as well as our personal lives tend to draw the greatness out of us and shake us out of our complacency. Challenge causes us to stretch and to let go of control. Challenge helps us discover our greatest gifts, highest capacities and our authentic selves.

Over the next 30 days, I gently offer you the following challenges:

- I challenge you to be a dreamer in a world, where too many people have given up on standing for their dreams.

- I challenge you to be the most positive person you know, in a world where negativity prevails and cynicism is considered cool.

- I challenge you to do 3 things that you are afraid to do (because your fears are portals into your best life) and visit the places that scare you.

- I challenge you to exercise regularly, eat impeccably and treat your body as a temple.

- I challenge you to be a better mate, a more loving parent and a more noble human being.

- I challenge you to spend 60 minutes every morning in a "Holy Hour", reflecting on what you want your life to stand for and reading from something deep and inspiring.

- I challenge you to devote yourself to excellence in a society where too many people accept mediocrity.

- I challenge you to be a light, on a planet filled with too much darkness, and to do good deeds daily – even if they go unrecognized.

I challenge you to make the choices available to you, to make this month an extraordinary month. I challenge you to take the words that I offered and to deeply reflect on them so that they inspire you to action. I challenge you to take one moment – right now – to remember who you truly are. Stand to be great.

INSPIRATIONAL QUOTES

"The smallest of actions is always better than the noblest of intentions".

Robin Sharma, "Who Will Cry When You Die?"

"Freedom is the only worthy goal in life. It is done by disregarding things that lie beyond our control. We cannot have a light heart if our minds are a woeful cauldron of fear..."

Epictetus, A Manual For Living

"The beauty of a soul shines out when a man bears with composure one heavy mischance after another, not because he does not feel them, but because he is a man of high temper."

Aristotle

6 WAYS TO BE A BETTER PARENT

1. Have a weekly "private date" with each one of your children so that you connect with them at a deeper level.

2. Develop a nightly practice of encouraging your children to write in a journal while you do the same.

3. Be silly with your children. Make the time to laugh, play and be spontaneous.

4. While you are driving your children to activities, have powerful conversations on meaningful topics such as character strength, goal-setting, standing for excellence and living your truth.

5. Be an "aggressive listener" with your children. In other words, listen deeply to what they have to say.

6. Tell your children how great they are and how much you love them on a frequent basis.

QUESTIONS TO JOURNAL ON

1. What do I love doing?

2. Who has been my greatest influence?

3. What would I die for?

4. What's most important to me?

5. What's holding me back?

HOW TO TRANSCEND FEAR

In my work with people from all around the world, I have discovered the primary reason people play small with their lives is that they are filled with fear. Each and every one of us has our own fears. Interestingly, most of us share the same fears: a fear of rejection, a fear of failure, a fear of not being good enough, a fear of being alone, a fear of losing control and a fear of success. At our transformational 2 day personal discovery weekend called Awakening Best Self (ABS), I share with participants a powerful process to help them release the fears that have limited them for most of their lives. One of the things that you can do today to move through your fears and play a bigger game as a human being is to begin to validate your fears and pay attention to them. Most of us deny our fears. We pretend that they are not there and structure our entire lives so that we don't have to face our fears. But when we face our fears, we not only grow in our personal power, but our fears feel heard. It is important to acknowledge your fears. Become aware of them. Even more effective is to put a voice to your fears. Talk about your fears. Have conversations with those you trust about the fears that are preventing you from the life of your dreams. When your fears are validated and recognized, they lose their power over you.

Journaling about your fears is also another valuable technique to help you transcend them. We all have a light side and a dark side and our fears live within the realm of our shadow selves. When you take a shadow and place it into the sunlight, it begins to dissolve. Similarly, when you take your shadow side (much of which is unconscious) and bring your fears into the light of your conscious awareness, they can begin to leave. Just imagine how gorgeous this world would look if most of us had the freedom to live without fear? Just imagine how much love there would be in the world if most of us were living lives that made us happy? Just imagine how great the world would be if we were letting our light shine as it was meant to shine?

19

The Eternal Quest for Happiness

⊙

SINCE THE BEGINNING of civilization, human beings have been seeking lasting happiness. Mystics pondered how one could find sustained joy, while living deep in the mountains. Philosophers wondered how a person could feel they were living their greatest lives no matter what was going on in their outer worlds. And modern day writers have offered many different theories on how a person can find contentment in a world where there has never been so much uncertainty and turbulence. Of course, I am no different from you: I seek happiness within every day of my life.

And just as I'm sure is the case with you, I have my good days as well as my bad days. I believe the real goal to strive for is to feel eternal peace and happiness on the inside no matter what is going on on the outside. By this I mean, we cannot control life – it will unfold according to its own logic. But you can control the way that you interpret and process what is going on externally for you. Why our lives unfold the way that they do is one of life's greatest mysteries. You exercise your own authentic power as a human being when you use everything that happens to you, the apparently positive as well as the seemingly negative, as a platform to fuel greater success, internal peace and happiness.

Happiness, as a human being, also comes from fundamentals that I know you already know of: living your life from a frame of reference where you are devoted to helping other people, living in a way that allows you to have loving relationships with all those who surround you, taking daily risks so that you grow into more of who you are meant to be and dedicating yourself to leaving a legacy so that you are more than merely successful – you are significant.

Deep within you, you already know the way to happiness in your life. Reading books, listening to authors speak and visiting retreats only helps you remember the truth that already resides within your heart. As the great philosopher Kahlil Gibran wrote in his strikingly beautiful book "The Prophet": "...of what can I speak save of that which is even now moving within your souls?" And often, what is deepest within our hearts, is revealed only through the experience of silence. Through the inner work I've done on my own personal path, I've come to realize that the highest possibilities of our lives are revealed within the quiet spaces of our lives. Over the coming 30 days, I invite you to carve out some time to be alone and to ponder the following big question of your life: "what needs to happen, over the course of my life, for me to feel authentically happy?" Once you start arriving at some of your answers, you can make those wonderfully important course corrections to reclaim your greatest life.

INSPIRATIONAL QUOTES

"This is the true joy in life, the being used for a purpose recognized by yourself as a mighty one... the being a force of nature instead of a feverish, selfish little clod of ailments and grievances complaining that the world will not devote itself to making you happy."

George Bernard Shaw

"To venture causes anxiety, but not to venture is to lose one's self... and to venture in the highest is precisely to be conscious of one's self."

Soren Kierkegard

"Our own life is the instrument of which we experiment with the truth."

Thich Nhat Hanh

"You realize your destiny when you serve the force that created you and have the courage to let the brilliance within you see the light of day."

Robin Sharma

QUESTIONS TO JOURNAL ON

1. What needs to happen, between now and the end of your lifetime, for you to feel that it was truly successful?

2. List the 25 things that make you happiest in your life (and then rededicate yourself to doing them more often to increase your internal levels of happiness and fulfillment).

3. How old would you be if you did not know how old you were?

5 WAYS TO BECOME A MASTER TIME
TACTICIAN

1. Get up at 5 am and take 30 minutes to envision and plan out your best day.

2. Replace watching the television with higher leverage activities.

3. Get good at saying no to things that are not important (versus trying to please everyone).

4. Take the time to journal on your life's priorities so you gain greater clarity and conviction.

5. Throughout your day, repeat the question: "what is the best use of my time right now, here in this moment?"

20

The 5 Golden Disciplines of Life Mastery

⊙

Over the next 90 days, integrate these 5 disciplines into your daily structure. "These routines have had a profound impact on the quality of my own life and I know they will do the same for you."

The 5 Golden Disciplines are:

1. Join the 5 O'Clock Club and get up early to gain a psychological advantage.

2. Spend 15 minutes planning, strategizing and creating a template for your day.

3. Read from the wisdom literature for 30 minutes at the beginning of your day.

4. Exercise for 30 minutes because in the healthy body lives the healthy mind.

5. End your day reflecting on your day's successes (and failures) so the next one is better. The whole idea behind human growth is to let your past serve you and to make certain that each day lifts you a little closer to your ideal self and towards your ideal life.

INSPIRATIONAL QUOTES

"The tragedy of life is not death but what we let die inside of us while we live."

Norman Cousins

"In the midst of winter, I found there was within me an invincible summer."

Albert Camus

"The greatest privilege of leadership is the chance to elevate lives."

Robin Sharma

"If everybody was satisfied with himself, there would be no heroes."

Mark Twain

"It is only when we truly know and understand that we have a limited time on earth – and that we have no way of knowing when our time is up – that we will begin to live each day to the fullest, as if it was the only one we had."

Elisabeth Kubler-Ross

6 WAYS TO DEEPEN YOUR HUMAN CONNECTION

If you have ever experienced one of my incredible live seminars, you have heard me say: "the deeper your relationships, the more effective your leadership because people will not follow you if they do not trust you and before someone will lend you a hand, you must touch their hearts." All true success in business – and in life – comes down to high-quality, trust-based relationships. Over the next 90 days, commit yourself to relationship excellence and watch your career and your life soar.

Here are 6 of my best lessons on relationship building:

1. Remember to say please and thank you (good manners connect human hearts).

2. Send out 3 handwritten letters or postcards every day for the rest of your life.

3. Be the first to say sorry when you have made a mistake.

4. Buy 20 copies of your favorite book and send them to those you care about.

5. Keep your little promises and honor your tiny commitments.

6. Be a masterful listener (as deep listening honors the person and says "I value you").

21

Monumental Moments

⊙

IT'S SO EASY to postpone living greatly. We quietly tell ourselves that we will travel more when the kids go off to university or that we will deepen relationships with loved ones when we reach a greater level of success in our careers or that we will do our dreams once we have more time. But your time is now. This day is your life.

An extraordinary life is nothing more than a series of outrageously well-lived minutes strung together like a necklace of pearls. Make each one of your moments monumental and your greatness – both at work and in life will be assured. Don't put off your best life. You'll get to the end before you know it. Seriously.

This can be your year. No, let me rephrase that: this will be your year. The year you reveal your brilliance. The year you get into

world-class health. The year you fall madly in love with life. And
make each one of your moments works of art. Keep shining.

INSPIRATIONAL QUOTES

"In the process of creating any greatness, breaking any new
ground, failure will happen."

Advertising guru Donny Deutsch in
"Often Wrong, Never in Doubt"

"I don't care to belong to any club that would have me
as a member."

Groucho Marx

"The person who attempts to do everything ultimately achieves
nothing. Focus precedes greatness."

Robin Sharma

WHY PLAN

Personal planning and goal-setting are not sexy topics. But they are incredibly important and central to an extraordinary experience of life. I see it time and time again amongst those who are the best of the best: lots of time spent articulating a clear and detailed vision for what the key areas of their lives will look like and then a written plan with the vision broken down into sequenced goals so that the vision isn't so overwhelming and so the big picture is neatly chunked into manageable steps to drive daily action. One of the best effects of planning that I've discovered is what it does to my mind. Let me put it this way: few things focus the mind as well as setting plans on to paper and then sequencing them into goals. The very act of doing it heightens your awareness as to what's most important. And with better awareness, you will make better choices. And as you make better choices, you are certain to experience better results. So today, give yourself a gift: take out a nice, crisp white sheet of paper. Sharpen a pencil. And then start writing about the life you want to create. It's a lot easier than you may think.

ON EXCELLENCE VERSUS PERFECTION

Top software companies don't wait until a program is perfect before they release it to the world. They make sure it works, of course. They are certain it is excellent, definitely. But they know it's not perfect. Sure it will have a few bugs but their logic is that it's better to get it out there than miss the window of opportunity available to them. Too many amongst us wait for perfection to occur, and in so doing, miss openings to get to our dreams. The years slip by unbelievably fast. Don't blink you'll be old. Do your juiciest goals now. Get started this very moment. Be excellent. Forget perfection. And don't wait. Please.

2 2

CLOSING THE GAP

⊙

CHILDREN COME TO us more highly evolved than adults to teach us the lessons we need to learn. More than ever, we learn from children. Children are the most imaginative, innocent, passion-filled, playful, fearless people on the planet. And they are the most fun. Last week, my seven year old daughter Bianca asked me: "Dad, when can you take me to Hamsterdam?"

If you've been to one of our Awakening Best Self Weekend (ABS) or to our two day leadership coaching process The Elite Performers Series, you know about the Integrity GapTM. Essentially, this is a mental model that will help you understand, at a deep level, the journey of life and how we can become more aligned with our biggest selves such that we experience the fulfillment we are all meant to experience. We are born perfect, full of love, potential, self-faith and brilliance. But from the moment we are born, we begin to walk away from our authentic nature and take on the false beliefs, limiting assumptions and fears of the world around us. Then, one day we wake up as adults and realize that we have betrayed ourselves and have no idea who we truly are. We then embark upon the Seeker's Journey in effort to remember who we once were. In many ways, the job of the leader is to become more childlike.

Authenticity is a word I'm hearing a lot these days when I go in to organizations across the world as a speaker, executive coach and consultant. Most of us are recognizing there is a call on our lives and each of us has a mission that we are meant to achieve through the work we do and via the lives we live. There is a giant search for meaning within the corporate world. People are no longer willing to sacrifice fulfillment for economic benefits. We want to go to work each day and know that we are making a contribution. We want to go to work each day and know we are growing and evolving as human beings. We want to go to work each day and have fun while feeling connected with those around us. Perhaps, above all else, we are looking for workplaces where it's safe to be human again.

For the coming 30 days, I invite you to do what's required to close any Integrity GapTM in your life such that you show up fully. Leaders are true to themselves. The giants who have walked the planet before us (the Gandhis, the Mandelas, the Mother Theresas), did not follow the crowd but marched to their own drumbeat. They were originals and conducted their lives according to their own values rather than by the values of the world around them. And in doing so, they grew great.

Inspirational Quotes

"These days, building companies that win big in the marketplace, that create value for their customers and shareholders and that operate in ways that bring out the best in employees and executives is not just smart business – it's also an obligation of leadership."

Editorial from Fast Company

"The thing is, we still live in a world that's filled with opportunity. In fact, we have more than an opportunity – we have an obligation. An obligation to spend our time doing great things. To find ideas that matter and to share them. To push ourselves and the people around us to demonstrate gratitude, insight and inspiration. To take risks and to make the world better by being amazing."

Seth Godin, Author of "Purple Cow"

"Each and every one of us has far more choices as to what we can make of our lives than we can currently imagine. Most of us are not alive to the possibilities that exist before our very eyes. So many of us are asleep at the wheel of our own lives, part numb, and part empty. This is not a platitude but a core truth. You are destined for greatness. Your greatness might manifest itself differently from another's greatness but that still does not mean that you are not meant to be great. Let your light shine. Walk towards your fears. Do the thing that you are most afraid to do. Be fully alive."

Robin Sharma

SUCCESS AND SIGNIFICANCE: THE TWIN IDEALS

Excellence is a beautiful word. The people who are standing for their highest lives all have a devotion to excellence. They are committed to excellence in their professional lives. They are committed to excellence in their relationships. They are committed to excellence in their adventure lives. And they are committed to excellence in their inner lives. Human beings have a need to keep reaching for something better. When we live within our comfort zones, we do not find lasting happiness because we are not living as we are meant to live. But when we are constantly evolving, risking, growing, dreaming, and stretching our personal frontiers, we find happiness in the process. This is because we are being true to ourselves.

For the next 30 days, keep reaching for excellence. At work, raise your standards. Ask yourself: "What would I be doing each day if I was truly excellent and the best in the world at what I did?" At home, be excellent in the way you communicate within the conversations you have with your partner and children. In your spiritual life, reflect on whether you are devoted to reaching for your higher self. The pursuit of excellence is a noble call. You've given gifts for a reason: to let them shine and to make the world a better place in the process.

23

GRATITUDE

⊙

ONE OF THE things I am working on in my life at this point is deepening my connection to a state of gratitude and reverence for all that surrounds me. More than ever, I consciously focus on the blessings in my life (especially the simple ones) and give thanks that they are there. I also express gratitude for the challenges that I face and the adversity that I have encountered, knowing that they serve primarily to teach me the lessons that I most need to learn. I would like to take this opportunity to thank you for being a part of our community of change missionaries and dedicated leaders. I am grateful for your support of my work, your belief in my message and for your willingness to consider the ideas I continue to present to you. I feel privileged to do what I do and I genuinely thank you.

INSPIRATIONAL QUOTES

"It is only when we forget all our learning that we begin
to know."

Henry David Thoreau

"There is a wick within you that is waiting to become the light
of your soul. When this inner flame burns brightly, you will feel a
magnificent awakening in your life."

Bradford Keeney

"Mankind has never achieved greatness but through suffering."

F. Robert De Lamennais

7 WAYS TO THINK, FEEL AND ACT LIKE AN ELITE PERFORMER

1. Keep your promises and make your word your bond.

2. Make time for weekly silence, stillness and reflection.

3. Connect with a cause that engages you emotionally.

4. Build a network of mentors, models and advocates.

5. Balance a sharp mind with a wide open heart.

6. Give what you most want to receive in your life.

7. Rise with the sun and envision the day made up of your highest choices and your best moves.

Questions to Journal On

The right question provokes the right answer. In my own life, I have found that it is often more helpful to spend my time meditating on a powerful question than searching for a specific answer. Creative questioning is one of the best ways to deepen yourself and to open up the doorway into who you truly are. I invite you to engage in the following five questions over the next 30 days:

1. If you were living a truly extraordinary life, what would it look like?

2. What are the three top priorities of your life and does the way your life looks right now reflect these priorities?

3. If you had 10 minutes left to live, what thoughts would go through your mind and what feelings would you experience?

4. If you could have dinner with anyone in the world tonight, who would it be and why?

5. If you could discover a symbol that reflected and stood for your best life, what would that symbol be?

24

A DEVOTION TO EXCELLENCE

⊙

ONE OF THE greatest acts of self-betrayal is denying who you truly are. Greatness as a human being is your birthright. Every person on the planet today is hardwired to live a life that reflects a sense of fearlessness, passion, mastery and compassion. When you deny this by accepting various forms of mediocrity in your life, you dishonor your highest self and the person that you were designed to be.

"Everyone has the power for greatness, not for fame but for greatness," noted Martin Luther King Jr. So much of the malaise and disappointment that many of us feel deep within our hearts comes from the fact that, at a core level, part of us knows that we are not living to our highest capacity. One of the fundamental mental models that I teach to my executive coaching clients as well as at our Awakening Best Self weekends is that of The Integrity Gap™. Simply stated, the greater the gap between the person that you are designed to become and the person that you are now presenting to the world, the less your life will work. To liberate enormous amounts of energy, creativity and potential, it is essential that you do what is required to close The Integrity Gap™, on a daily basis. In doing so, you will be true to yourself. In making this effort, you will be far more authentic – professionally, personally, and spiritually.

I invite you to engage in a very powerful exercise: sometime today-before you go to sleep – take out a piece of paper and write down 5 Devotions for your professional life. These are 5 things that you will stand for, no matter what happens, within the realm of your professional work. These might be "impeccable integrity", "relentless innovation", "being the kindest person that I know" or "living each day as if it was my last." Then, set 5 Devotions for your personal life such as "no matter what happens, I will take 30 minutes to exercise each day" or "no matter how busy I get, I will always spend quality time each day with my mate and my children" or "no matter what comes up, I will begin each day at 5 a.m. with a period of silent reflection so that I can live life on my own terms." Making these kinds of commitments will alter the course of your destiny. "In one bold stroke you can transform today," wrote Marilyn Grey.

INSPIRATIONAL QUOTES

"Thought allied fearlessly to purpose becomes creative force; those who know this are ready to become something higher and stronger than mere bundles of wavering thoughts and fluctuating sensations."

James Allen, "As A Man Thinketh"

"That it will never come again is what makes life so sweet."

Emily Dickinson

"You can have anything you want if you want it desperately enough. You must want it with an exuberance that erupts through the skin and joins the energy that created the world."

Sheila Graham

"Leadership requires great courage. It is tough to leave the gravitational pull of the crowd around us. It is tough to take the road less traveled when everyone urges you to be like everyone else. It is tough to create your life on your own terms when others are telling you how your life should be created. But nothing will fill your heart with a greater sense of regret than lying on your deathbed knowing that you did not live your life and do your dreams."

Robin Sharma

6 WAYS TO AWAKEN YOUR BEST SELF

1. Write out a 1 paragraph statement, in your journal, clarifying what your life would look like if you were living the highest version of your highest vision.

2. Make it a personal standard, that you will never neglect to speak only truth – in all situations.

3. Refuse to give up on your dreams. In so many of our seminars and coaching intensives, when I ask participants what their # 1 regret is they respond: "so many years have passed by and I have not faced my dreams." Do not let this happen to you.

4. Do the inner-work required to get to know your fears. Once you know your fears, run toward them each day rather than running away from them. Your fears are portals into your greatest self. Every time a fear presents itself on the path of your life, realize that this is a giant opportunity to remember more of who you are truly meant to be and reclaim more of your authentic power as a human being.

5. Celebrate the small pleasures of life. At the end of our lives, we will realize that the small pleasures were actually the largest ones.

6. Become the most loving person you know, not just at home but at work. The people whose funerals attract standing-room only situations at churches, temples, mosques and synagogues were generally not those who had the most money in their bank accounts but those who had the most love within their hearts.

2 5

REINVENT YOURSELF

⊙

A NUMBER OF years ago I was on a flight with a well known
leadership consultant who happened to strike up a conversation
with me. Near the end of our time together, I asked him the
following question: "what has made you, and the organization
that you lead, so successful?" I'll never forget his response:
"Robin," he said, "my company and I are fearless when it comes
to consistent reinvention." He explained that every few years,
he reinvents himself. He takes a risk and then tries something
completely new in terms of the way he thinks, works and lives.
He told me that this ensured that all aspects of his life remained
exciting, fulfilling and fresh. He also informed me that this
attitude and best practice kept his clients engaged, because he
continually brought cutting-edge ideas to them.

What are you doing to reinvent yourself? What are you doing to push your personal frontiers and live a greater life? What are you doing to challenge the way you have always done things and to play a bigger game as a human being? What will you do to Dream, Dare, Shine?

INSPIRATIONAL QUOTES

"Nurture your mind with great thoughts, for you will never go any higher than you think."

Benjamin Disraeli

"The price of greatness is responsibility."

Winston Churchill

"That it will never come again is what makes life so sweet."

Emily Dickinson,

"Each one of us can elevate the world, one leader – one human being at a time. Walk out into the world today and bring more of your humanity, potential and greatness to everything that you do... and to each life that you touch. Sustained happiness comes not from what we get but through what we give."

Robin Sharma

The Price of Leadership

The difference between the best of the best and the also – rans in life is that genuine leaders consistently do what is right rather than what is easy. Authentic success does take hard work and self-discipline. In order to get to your greatest life, both professionally and personally, it's essential that you are willing to pay the price. Here are four simple ideas that will help you create spectacular results:

1. Raise your standards. Devote yourself to becoming world-class in all that you do. Expect nothing but the best from yourself. Our expectations create our reality.

2. Be the most positive person you know. Your passion is contagious. It's not easy to be positive when things get tough but that is part of what genuine leadership is about.

3. Remember that your health is your wealth. Without energy, you will never be able to realize your dreams and live your greatest life. Exercise. Eat well. And remember that your health is your most precious possession.

4. Make a difference. The deepest need of the human heart is to live for something more important than oneself. Leave people better than you found them. Give your best to your organization. And don't do it just for the organization – do it for yourself.

QUESTIONS TO JOURNAL ON

1. Where do you want to grow in your life?

2. If you were asked to describe yourself in one paragraph, what would that paragraph say?

3. Who are you?

4. If you could have dinner with 5 extraordinary people, who would they be and why?

5. What frustrates you the most in your life and what could you do to eliminate this frustration?

26

ARE YOU GOOD?

⊙

I HAVE BEEN spending a lot of time lately thinking about the fundamentals of greatness. I've been reflecting on some of the simpler attributes that separate the most unforgettable men and women who have graced this planet from the rest. We live in an age where complexity is sexy and we seek out sophisticated strategies and tactics that will help us to become more successful at work and in our lives. But deep within our hearts, we know that authentic success is a simple process. Yes, we must be excellent at what we do. Yes, our products and services must be world-class. Yes, we must develop a high-performance team. Yes, we must build an architecture of execution so that the most important things get done. But more than anything else, I believe that to be truly great, we must be good.

People love doing business with good people. And yet, in this age of great ambiguity and relentless change, so many people cut "ethical corners". Too many people think that dishonesty will get them ahead. Too many people have forgotten the importance of using words like "please" and "thank you". Too many people think that if you are nice, you will be eaten alive in today's marketplace. But being ethical, compassionate and dedicated to adding enormous value to those around you is probably the best way to ensure your success. In the words of Robert Louis Stevenson: "everybody, soon and late, sits down to a banquet of consequences."

Here are a few simple ideas to help you continue to raise your "Goodness Quotient":

• Be the most polite person that you know.

• Be honest to a fault.

• Deeply commit yourself to being a world-class listener.

• Send handwritten thank you notes on a regular basis.

• Seek out opportunities to do random acts of kindness.

• Commit yourself to being the most positive and passionate person that you know.

• Be impeccable with your punctuality.

Success and leadership come down to simple fundamentals that elite performers practice on a daily basis. The latest business books offer sophisticated ideas and cutting – edge suggestions.

But to be truly great, stick to the basics that you know in your heart are most important. Be kind. Be excellent. Be passionate. And more than anything else, be good.

INSPIRATIONAL QUOTES

"You will make more friends in two months by being interested in other people than you will in two years by trying to get people interested in you."

Dale Carnegie

"Each man had only one genuine vocation – to find the way to himself...his task was to discover his own destiny – not an arbitrary one – and live it out wholly and resolutely within himself. Everything else was only a would be existence, an attempt at evasion, a flight back to the ideals of the masses, conformity and fear of one's own inwardness."

Herman Hesse, in Demian

"Practice small daily acts of greatness. A great life is nothing more than a series of well lived days strung together like a necklace of pearls. Every day, wake up and commit yourself to being excellent, being innovative and being good over the coming hours. This strategy alone will ensure your authentic success."

Robin Sharma

7 WAYS TO BOOST YOUR ENERGY

1. Exercise for 30 minutes 4 times a week.

2. Spend time in nature on a weekly basis.

3. Don't eat after 8:00 pm.

4. Get a massage every week.

5. Eat an elite performance diet, completely cutting out junk food.

6. Read something inspiring for 30 minutes first thing every morning (it will energize you).

7. Drink lots of water.

QUESTIONS TO JOURNAL ON

1. If you could have five famous friends, who would they be?

2. Who do you most admire in your life and why?

3. What does excellence look like in your life?

4. What three things could you do to be a more loving person?

5. What five things will likely happen if you do not get into excellent physical condition?

Are you Devoted to Lifelong Learning

When I was growing up, my father encouraged me to read on a daily basis. He believed that reading a book was nothing more than having a conversation with the author. And like any good conversation, when you walk away from it, you begin to see the world through a new set of eyes. Thanks to my father's instruction, I've developed a deep love of reading and a serious hunger for knowledge. I'm certainly not perfect but one of the things that I do right in my life is remain curious and open to new ideas.

How much time do you spend reading? Too many people in the world today spend more time watching television than they do nurturing their intellectual base. And yet, we live in a world where ideas are the commodity of success. The most successful and fulfilled people are those who think the best thoughts. We can only act on what we know. And when we know better, we can choose better.

27

BUILD A GREAT DAY

⊙

As I TEACH in my corporate leadership seminars: "a great life is nothing more than a series of days well lived strung together like a string of pearls. Focus on building great days and a great life is sure to follow." Here are 6 ways to ensure that every day is a brilliant one:

1. Begin your day by writing down 10 things you have to be grateful for in your life.

2. Take 30 minutes and read from the wisdom literature to restore your perspective and inspire your self.

3. Take 5 minutes and plan your day, thereby creating a template that you can live the remaining hours out of. Also set 3 small goals that you will achieve this day "no matter what."

4. Eat the kind of breakfast that an athlete training for the event of her life would eat and drink plenty of water to stay in your peak state.

5. At the end of your day, reflect on how you have spent your day by writing in your journal. Evaluate your actions and detect areas where you need to improve.

6. End your day on a high note by thinking about the "small wins" of your day (i.e., promises you kept, the workout you enjoyed, the relationship you built, the lesson you learned or the insight you had).

Inspirational Quotes

"We should be careful to get out of an experience only the wisdom that is in it – and stop there; lest we be like the cat that sits down on a hot stove lid. It will never sit down on a hot stove lid again – and that is well; but also it will never sit down on a cold one anymore."

Mark Twain

"Life is short. Do not forget about the most important things in our life, living for other people and doing good for them."

Marcus Aurelius

"The greatest irony of leadership is that the more you give, the more you get. And when all is said and done, the highest and most enduring gift that you will ever be able to give is the gift of what you leave behind. Your legacy to the generations that follow you will be the value you have added and the lives you have improved."

Robin Sharma,
"Leadership Wisdom from the Monk Who Sold His Ferrari"

5 WAYS TO BE A LEADER AT HOME

1. Organize and then ritualize (i.e., institutionalize) a daily family meal. At this meal, go around the table and ask each family member what they learned during their day and what they might do tomorrow to make it even better.

2. Be the model. You can't really teach leadership – you can only model it. With your family, be a shining example of the ideal you expect of others.

3. Create a learning culture. In my work with corporations, I teach employees how they can contribute to the creation of a learning culture so that innovation and ideas rule the day. In your home environment, take action to shape a culture that fosters learning and the sharing of wisdom and knowledge. This might mean that you bring home a book from the wisdom literature and discuss it on a Sunday afternoon or simply turn off the TV and engage your family in some deep, heart-to-heart dialogue.

4. Connect hearts. The richest human connection occurs when we connect to the heart of another. This means we see the world through their eyes and care about the needs that drive them. It means we resolve to be there for them in the tough times and celebrate with them in the good ones. It means we have the self-discipline to listen in a soulful way and recognize them when they make improvements. It means that we truly give love to them.

5. Be a light. What we need more of on this planet are people who are lights: men and women who are aware that every human being can make a positive difference and elevate the lives of others through the leadership they show. Dedicate yourself to being the best you can be, raising your standards and living in a way that transcends yourself. The world will be better for it.

THE VALUE OF KEEPING A LIFE JOURNAL

One of the most important disciplines I keep to stay at my best is journaling. I started this practice about 10 years ago and wish I'd done it sooner. I really want you to live your best life and engage in the process of living fully – writing in a journal every

few days will help you do this. Here are some of the benefits
I get from journaling:

1. Capture. Within the pages of my journal (a $5 coil bound
notebook), I capture great ideas that I want to study and then
integrate into my life. If I'm reading the newspaper and someone
makes an interesting point, I'll cut out the quote and paste it in the
journal. Then I'll write my own insights under it (I fly a lot and
always carry my journal, a pair of scissors and a glue stick in my
briefcase). If there is a picture of one of my heroes in a magazine or
an image relating to one of my goals, again, I cut it out and paste it
in. This very act floods me with hope and keeps my dreams alive.

2. Consolidate. I find that, as a serious student of the process
of living, I need to write things down to really connect with
them. Here's what I mean: if I attend a seminar or read a great
book, I find that by writing down what I've learned, the lessons
go deeper within me. They become far more integrated and I
remember them far more clearly.

3. Release. If I've had a challenging day, I pull out my journal
and "dump out" my frustrations and express my experiences on
paper. This very act releases stress and makes me feel the way I'd
feel after speaking deeply with my best friend.

4. Reflect. As I wrote in my book "Leadership Wisdom from
The Monk Who Sold His Ferrari: The 8 Rituals of Visionary
Leaders", "reflection is the mother of wisdom." We live in a

world where people no longer carve out some time every week to do nothing but think. Yet, if you fail to reflect deeply on the way you are conducting your life and make those all-important course corrections, you are certain to make the same mistakes over and over again. My journal offers me a place to have a conversation with myself and do some personal introspection. In doing so, my past serves me and every day builds on the previous one.

28

What Makes an Elite
Performer?

⊙

OUR 2 DAY corporate coaching program, The Elite
Performers Series, has yielded stunning success with our
corporate clients which have included major banks, one of
the world's largest software companies and manufacturing
organizations. Based upon our proprietary process of Emotion
Centric Leadership, the program causes employees to think, feel
and act as elite performers and authentic leaders. In this age of
whitewater change, it is easy for employees to forget what truly
counts. With all the distractions that appear within our days, it
is so easy for us to forget to play our highest game and let our true
talents shine through. With all that is on our plates in this age of
speed, technology and uncertainty, it is easy to forget what elite
performance looks like and the imperative placed upon each of us
to fulfill our greatest potential as people.

Living and working at the standard of an elite performer makes us feel good about ourselves. Within each and every one of us is a witness. By this I mean, we each, deep within our core, have a place of knowing that watches how we live and conduct our lives. When we live according to our genuine values, work hard, treat people well and add value through the work that we do, this witness watches and sees that we are being true to our original nature. Our self-respect increases and our lives cannot help but work. We begin to feel better about ourselves. Energy is released and we become more of who we truly are. Committing yourself to elite performance in every dimension of your life does not add to the complexity of your days. Instead, it will raise the quality of your life and simplify things for you. And deep within us, we have a human hunger to actualize our highest gifts and become the people we are destined to be. Yet, most of us fail to accept this calling. We play small lives and fall into the trap of believing that greatness is reserved for the chosen few. One of my deepest beliefs is that everyone on the planet belongs to the tribe of the "chosen few". Every one on this planet has a brilliance within them that would startle them if they accessed it. As Fredrick Faust once wrote: "there is a giant asleep within everyone. When that giant awakens, miracles happen."

As we enter the summer months, I invite you to make the time to become more reflective. Keep paying attention to how you are living and the levels at which you perform. Keep asking yourself questions such as: "am I fulfilling my potential?", "am I resisting personal greatness?", "is what I am doing in my days creating a rich legacy?". Perhaps, you might choose to spend more time in nature. Perhaps, you might engage in deeper conversations around the meaning of elite performance and the value that it will bring to your life. If there is one thing I know it is this: the world needs more leaders. The world needs people playing their highest game and living their best lives. The world needs people who are lights and individuals who believe in the brilliance that every human being is meant to reflect. Open your heart to elite performance and make a series of heartfelt commitments that will help you step into the next possibility of your business and personal life. To do this will be a noble gesture on your part.

INSPIRATIONAL QUOTES

"Life is short. Do not forget about the most important things in life, living for other people and doing good for them."

Marcus Aurelius

"Do not regret the past. What is the use of regrets? The lie says that you should regret. The truth says that you should be filled with love. Push all sad memories away from you. Do not speak of the past. Live in the light of love, and all things will be given to you."

Persian wisdom

"It is only when we forget all our learning that we begin to know."

Henry David Thoreau

"The duty of the leader is not to self-improve but to self-remember. You already are everything you've ever dreamed of being. By doing the inner work required to know yourself, you will access your authentic power and reclaim who you truly are. This is what personal awakening is all about. This is the essence of life. This is the secret to success. This is what true leaders do."

Robin Sharma

3 QUESTIONS TO JOURNAL ON

1. If your life could stand for one word, what would that one word be, and why?

2. What has been the defining moment of your life and how did it serve to shape, sculpt and develop you?

3. What are you most resisting in your life at this moment?

The Beauty of Fear

Do you visit the places that scare you on a daily basis? Do you run towards your fears rather than running away from them? All leaders understand that on the other side of their fears lives their fortune. If you resist your fears, they will persist. But if you embrace them and run directly toward them, you will be walking directly towards your growth as a human being. Your fears actually represent opportunities to get to know yourself at a deeper level. Your fears are nothing more than your growth coming to get you. When you know your fears, you know the work that needs to be done to reclaim your authentic power. For example, if you have a fear of being vulnerable and you run away from it, that fear will always play a lead role in your life. On the other hand, if you have the courage to walk towards that fear and step into it (and move through it), you will have made a giant step towards being more of who you truly are. You will have transcended a fear and in doing so, become more powerful as a person and as a leader. Remember, fears are signposts that reflect opportunities to become more powerful and more authentic. Visit them daily and get to know them. They are not as scary as you might think.

29

BUILD YOUR AWARENESS

⊙

ONE OF THE primary ways we can change our lives and show up fully as leaders is to build awareness around the things that truly count. The more conscious you can become about your priorities, your desires and the areas you need to improve, the more positive change will occur in your life. Limiting beliefs, false assumptions and negative habits begin to lose their hold over you when they are placed into the light of awareness. Here are five questions to build your awareness around over the next month:

1. What would my life look like if I was living as I know I have the potential to live?

2. Who are three people who, if I really got to know them, could help me lift my life to the next level?

3. What 3 books could I read to inspire me to create my beautiful life?

4. What one thing could I do each week to lift my life to its highest level?

5. What is the single most limiting factor that is keeping me from living the life my heart desires?

INSPIRATIONAL QUOTES

"Accountability is the opportunity to live at choice rather than accidentally. Accountability is the opportunity to carve out the future rather than to sit back and have it happen to you. Accountability held from a stand as one's word is the ground from which one's own transformation is created ongoingly."

Werner Erhard

"I don't know what your destiny will be, but one thing I do know: the only ones among you who will really be happy are those who have sought and found how to serve."

Albert Schweitzer

"There is a giant asleep within everyone. When that giant awakens, miracles happen."

Frederick Faust

5 WAYS TO LET YOUR INNER SELF SHINE

1. Be the most authentic person that you know so that the person you present to the world reflects the person you are on the inside.

2. Become the kindest person that you know.

3. Speak your truth in all instances (but do it in a loving way).

4. Live each day within an awareness of your mortality.

5. Be more concerned about the happiness of others than the happiness of yourself.

30

LEADERSHIP CHALLENGE

⊙

IN THE MOVIE ROUNDERS, Pappa Wallenda, the famed highwire walker, said: "life is lived out on the wire. The rest is just waiting." All the joy, possibility and festivity of your life lies just beyond your fear doors. Daily risk taking is a powerful way to move into the higher places of your life. Never forget that on the other side of all your fears lies all your freedom. Today, take five minutes and do a Fear Audit listing every single one of the fears that is preventing your bigness as a human being from shining through. Then, over the next 30 days, do something small but uncomfortable to tackle these fears (which are really nothing more than imaginary limitations you have constructed as you have journeyed through life). Feel the fear and do it anyway. Something remarkable will start to shift within you over the next few weeks. Confidence will grow and momentum will inspire you to conquer even more of your fears.

INSPIRATIONAL QUOTES

"The place where your greatest fears live is also the place where your greatest growth lies."

Robin Sharma

"To live in hearts we leave behind is not to die."

Thomas Campbell

"Ask your heart 'If my life were only a little bit longer, what is most important, what do I value, how do I want to live?"

Jack Kornfield

"Stop playing small with your life. Tackle your fears, let go of the past and reach deep into your heart to reconnect with the person you were destined to be. Then go out into the world today and do something small to make it a better place."

Robin Sharma

5 Ways to be Your Best Self

1. Be consistently compassionate. No one ever wished they had been less kind on their deathbed. The most important thing you can do to live a greater life is to act, speak and live from your heart. Only then will your universe change.

2. Be humble. Live with what the Eastern sages call the beginners mind. Remember that everyone who enters your life has a story to tell and a lesson to teach if you have the wisdom to be open to it. Also remember that everyone who comes into your life does so at exactly the right time to teach you the lesson you most needed to learn.

3. Get good at being uncomfortable. The joy of life lives in living your life out on the skinny branch. Stop craving security and staying within your small zone of complacency. Dream bolder dreams. Meet wiser people. Do greater things. Cultivate the action habit by never leaving the site of a new idea without doing something to bring it to life.

4. Be a relationship builder and a light in this world. The richer your relationships, the richer a person you will be. Happiness as a human being comes, in large part, from the degree of connection we feel to the people in our lives. Really really happy people work really really hard on their "human connections". Over the next 30 days, ask yourself how you can be more of a light to the people you surround yourself with. Perhaps you might commit to smiling more or trusting more or serving more. If you want more love in your life the solution is simple: be more loving. Remember – to have more in life, you must first become more to the world.

5. Do the inner work. All leadership in life begins with leadership of self. Stop hoping that your life will change if only the people around you will change. Set about to improve the person that you are and watch good things start happening to you. Read for 30 minutes every day. Keep a journal so you become more deliberate in the way you govern your days. Respect your time. Nurture your body. Commune with nature and commit from your core to elevating the way you think, feel and live.

31

LEAD WITHOUT TITLE

⊙

OVER THE PAST few months, I have been traveling to many different countries sharing a simple message with organizations: everyone – from the CEO to the person on the front line – needs to think, feel and behave like a leader. I deeply believe that a company's competitive advantage comes down to its ability to develop the leadership capacities of its people faster than their competition. Leadership is not just for people who work in the executive suite. No matter what you do within an organization (or in your community), if you consume oxygen, you have the opportunity to show leadership. And this world needs human beings behaving like leaders more than ever before. Simply put, each of us needs to lead without title if we hope to get to greatness.

Many business executives ask me what genuine leadership looks like. To me, leadership means taking personal responsibility for results. Leadership means you get things done. Leadership means you keep your promises. Leadership means you see the best in people and coach them to success. Leadership means you are the most positive person you know and an individual dedicated to building relationships. Leadership means you have a sense of social responsibility so that you not only get your organization to world-class but you do your part to build a new world. And leadership ultimately means that, rather than cursing the darkness, you light a candle.

Just imagine what this world would look like if each one of us demonstrated our natural leadership abilities. People would no longer be playing victim. People would be using their natural creativity to produce brilliant results. People would be helping others realize their potential and make a difference through their lives. Organizations would become extraordinary. Communities would become extraordinary. And this world of ours would be a vastly improved place.

Inspirational Quotes

"Great companies have a lot in common with great teams. Players who practice hard when no one is paying attention generally play hard when everyone's watching. Success at any level can be reverse engineered to reveal the same architecture."

Michael Jordan

"The first step to becoming extraordinary is to simply stop being ordinary."

Seth Godin

"Health is the crown on a well man's head that only the sick man can see."

Anonymous

"As you live your days, so you craft your life."

Robin Sharma

DON'T GIVE UP

Sitting here in a Starbucks. Drinking coffee. Thinking. Not daydreaming. Not wasting time. Not worrying. Simply thinking. One of my best habits. Mostly I'm thinking about the importance of having a sense of mission and then staying true to it. It's not easy though.

I've found that the bigger I dream, the more obstacles I face. My mission in life is pretty straightforward: I want to help human beings become extraordinary and organizations get to world-class. I have such passion to get that dream done and do my part to make this world a better place. This isn't just a business to me – it's my calling. But the higher I reach, the more I get tested. Sound familiar?

But challenges are good. We grow through them. We are most alive amidst danger. The wisest amongst us – the genuine leaders, smile in the face of adversity. They understand that life tests the big dreamers – the passionate revolutionaries. It's almost like a weeding out process – only the strong (and the best) get to live their heart song.

So I'll rise above any resistance I meet. I'll keep my eyes on the dream. I'll stay on message and solidly on mission. Because this world belongs to us dreamers – you and I. And whether we ultimately win or not, we will have made a difference. And that's good enough for me.

3 2

THE POWER OF PERSPECTIVE

⊙

LAST MONTH, I spent three days in India in preparation for
the production of "The Monk Who Sold His Ferrari" as a major
motion picture. As I met various people in that great land of so
many different cultures, I was provided with an opportunity to
regain perspective. I was reminded that, no matter where I go in
the world, human beings still struggle with the same challenges.
No matter who I meet, we all have the same longings. No matter
who I connect with, I've come to understand that we are all part
of one great family with invisible ties.

During the summer months, I invite you to take time out for
yourself to restore perspective. It may be valuable for you to find
the time to list your blessings and write gratitude letters to people
who have made your life what it currently is. Perhaps, pick up the

phone and have a series of conversations with individuals who have enriched your life and helped you when you most needed help. You may also reflect on how fortunate you are in a world where many people are struggling to simply survive. As you take an inventory of your life, think about the books that have shaped your thinking and the movies that have inspired you. Think about the people that you have worked with that have made your life better as well as the experiences that have defined you.

It is so easy to fall into the trap of being so busy living your life that you never take the time to work on your life. During these quieter months, it might be valuable to reflect on what it is you want to create over the coming years and how you will breathe life into your dreams. Reflect on what's working in your life and what's not working in your life. Ponder the things that are excellent about your life and the things that do not align with your commitment to being truly world-class in all that you do. And remember, the world will be less of a place if you do not play your biggest game as a human being.

Inspirational Quotes

"There can be no progress, no achievement, without a certain degree of sacrifice, and our worldly success will be directly proportional to the degree that we overcome selfish, indulgent thoughts and fix our minds on the development of our plans and the strengthening of our resolution and self-reliance."

James Allen

"With all its shame, drudgery and broken dreams, it is still a beautiful world. Be cheerful. Strive to be happy."

Desiderata

"Two men look out through the same bars; one sees the mud and the other sees the stars."

Frederick Langbridge

"When you live your truth, your dreams beat a path toward your doorstep."

Robin Sharma

QUESTIONS TO JOURNAL ON

1. Success without significance is a hollow victory.

2. Nothing great was ever accomplished without hard work and significant sacrifice.

3. The bigger the risk, the bigger the rewards.

4. Good things happen when you do good things for others.

you are meant to be? Authentic leadership is all about being the person you know in your heart you have always been destined to be. Authentic leadership does not come from your title or from the size of your paycheck. Instead, this form of leadership comes from your being and the person that you are.

Here are 10 things that authentic leaders do on a regular basis:

1. They speak their truth. In business today, we frequently 'swallow our truth'. We say things to please others and to look good in front of the crowd. Authentic leaders are different. They consistently talk truth. They would never betray themselves by using words that are not aligned with who they are. This does not give anyone a license to say things that are hurtful to people. Speaking truth is simply about being clear, being honest and being authentic.

2. They lead from the heart. Business is about people. Leadership is about people. The best leaders wear their hearts on their sleeves and are not afraid to show their vulnerability. They genuinely care about other people and spend their days developing the people around them. They are like the sun: the sun gives away all it has to the plants and the trees. But in return, the plants and the trees always grow toward the sun.

3. They have rich moral fiber. Who you are speaks far more loudly than anything you could ever say. Strength of character is true power – and people can feel it a mile away. Authentic leaders work on their character. They walk their talk and are aligned with their core values. They are noble and good. And in doing so, people trust, respect and listen to them.

4. They are courageous. It takes a lot of courage to go against the crowd. It takes a lot of courage to be a visionary. It takes a lot of inner strength to do what you think is right even though it may not be easy. We live in a world where so many people walk the path of least resistance. Authentic leadership is all about taking the road less traveled and doing, not what is easy, but what is right.

5. They build teams and create communities. One of the primary things that people are looking for in their work experience is a sense of community. In the old days, we got our community from where we lived. We would have block parties and street picnics. In the new age of work, employees seek their sense of community and connection from the workplace. Authentic leaders create workplaces that foster human linkages and lasting friendships.

6. They deepen themselves. The job of the leader is to go deep. Authentic leaders know themselves intimately. They nurture a strong self-relationship. They know their weaknesses and play to their strengths. And they always spend a lot of time transcending their fears.

7. They are dreamers. Einstein said that: "imagination is more important than knowledge." It is from our imaginations that great things are born. Authentic leaders dare to dream impossible dreams. They see what everyone else sees and then dream up new possibilities. They spend a lot of time with their eyes closed creating blueprints and fantasies that lead to better products, better services, better workplaces and deeper value. How often do you close your eyes and dream?

8. They care for themselves. Taking care of your physical dimension is a sign of self-respect. You can't do great things at work if you don't feel good. Authentic leaders eat well, exercise and care for the temples that are their bodies. They spend time in nature, drink plenty of water and get regular massages so that, physically, they are operating at planet-class levels of performance.

9. They commit to excellence rather than perfection. No human being is perfect. Every single one of us is a work in progress. Authentic leaders commit themselves to excellence in everything that they do. They are constantly pushing the envelope and raising their standards. They do not seek perfection and have the wisdom to know the difference. What would your life look like if you raised your standards well beyond what anyone could ever imagine of you?

10. They leave a legacy. To live in the hearts of the people around you is to never die. Success is wonderful but significance is even better. You were made to contribute and to leave a mark on the people around you. In failing to live from this frame of reference, you betray yourself. Authentic leaders are constantly building their legacies by adding deep value to everyone that they deal with and leaving the world a better place in the process.

QUESTIONS TO JOURNAL ON

1. If your life could stand for one word, what would that one word be, and why?

2. What has been the defining moment of your life and how did it serve to shape, sculpt and develop you?

3. What are you most resisting in your life at this moment?

34

RENEWAL THROUGH TRAVEL

☉

IN MY MIND, the purpose of life is all about learning, growth
and reclaiming the authentic power that resides within us.
Traveling is one of the best ways to grow both professionally as
well as personally as it offers you the opportunity to step out of
the safe harbor of your daily routine, renew your perspective, be
exposed to new ideas and confront your resistances.

I have just returned from a 2 week tour of Europe and Israel, during
which I filled 2 leather-bound journals with ideas, reflections
and insights. The trip has renewed me, inspired me and caused
me to re-dedicate myself to living my highest game as a human
being. In London, I stayed at St. Martin's Lane, a hotel owned by
Ian Schrager (the former Studio 54 owner who has reinvented
himself as a boutique hotelier). Visiting St. Martin's Lane is a case

study in innovation and an extraordinary example of creativity in business. As you enter the elevators you are immediately struck by a video screen of a man's eyes staring at you. The experience continues with the unique music playing both in the elevator and in the hallways. As you enter the room, you cannot help but notice that you can customize the lighting in your room to your specific taste including the various colors which range from purple to red to green and blue. Not only is St. Martin's Lane remarkable for the experience it creates, its service levels are also among the best I've experienced. Next, in Amsterdam, I visited the Anne Frank museum which was a moving tribute to the power of one person to be a force for good in the world. In Paris, I was flooded with a stream of ideas upon visiting the Salvador Dali museum, a man who not only thought outside the box – he blew the box up and swallowed the pieces. A truly remarkable artist and a genius in his own right. In Florence, I watched the sun rise over the Duomo and experienced some of the world's most precious works of art at the Museum of Uffizi. In Rome, I watched the sun set over the Coliseum and was reminded of the ancient Roman's devotion to excellence in everything they do from physical fitness to philosophy.

Finally, in Israel I was deeply moved by the sacred sites in Jerusalem and the adventurer within me was delighted when I had the opportunity to float in the Dead Sea and view the cave where the original Dead Sea Scrolls were first discovered. Whether you take a year off to sail or a long weekend to reconnect with a loved one, travel will renew you, inspire you and excite you to be the best that you were meant to be. Today, make a choice to read more, attend a seminar that will help you realize your highest potential and do whatever it takes to stretch yourself beyond your current zone of safety. As Carl Jung once said: "where the fear is falling, the only safety lies in jumping."

INSPIRATIONAL QUOTES

"To do harm is to do yourself harm. To do an injustice is to do yourself an injustice – it degrades you."

Meditations of Marcus Aurelius

"We are earth people on a spiritual journey to the stars. Our quest, our earth walk, is to look within, to know who we are, to see that we are connected to all things, there is no separation, only in the mind."

Native American saying

"You were meant for greatness. When you play small with your life, you dishonor not only yourself but the force that created you."

Robin Sharma

"Most of us are anxious to improve our circumstances but are unwilling to improve ourselves – and we therefore remain bound."

James Allen, "As A Man Thinketh"

QUESTIONS TO JOURNAL ON

1. Am I playing my highest game as a human being?

2. Am I confronting my resistances and walking towards my fears?

3. Am I living my life or am I living the life that those around me wish me to live?

4. What needs to happen between now and the end of the year for me to feel that I am a success?

5. What are the 3 most important things in my life and am I focusing on these?

35

LIFE WISDOM TO ENRICH YOUR PATH

☉

THE FOLLOWING IS an excerpt from my bestseller "Who Will Cry When You Die?" (available at www.robinsharma.com or good book stores everywhere).

On being asked about the ups and downs of his career, movie star Kevin Costner responded with these words, "I am living a life." I found this reply to be profound. Rather than spending your days judging the events and experiences of his life as either good or bad, he adopted a neutral stance and simply decided to accept them for what they are: a natural part of the path he is on.

We all travel different roads to our ultimate destinations. For some of us, the path is rockier than for others. But no one reaches the end without some form of adversity. And the purpose of adversity is to improve us. So rather than fight it, why not accept it as the way of life? Why not detach yourself from the outcome and simply experience every circumstance that enters your life to the fullest? Feel the pain and savor the happiness. If you have never visited the valley, then the view of the mountain top is not as breathtaking. Remember, there are no real failures in life, only results. There are no true tragedies, only lessons. And there are really no problems, only opportunities for growth waiting to be recognized as solutions by the person of wisdom.

INSPIRATIONAL QUOTES

"Few will have the greatness to bend history itself but each one of us can work to change a small portion of events, and in the total of all those acts will be written the history of this generation."

Robert F. Kennedy

"There comes a special moment in everyone's life, a moment for which that person was born. That special opportunity, when he seizes it, will fulfill his mission – a mission for which this person is uniquely qualified. In that moment, we find our greatness. It is our finest hour."

Winston Churchill

"Far away in the sunshine are my highest aspirations. I may not reach them, but I can look up and see their beauty, believe in them, try to follow them."

Louisa May Alcott

The 3 Final Questions of Life

At the end of your life, when you strip away all the accessories that are important to us now, only 3 things will be important:

1. Have you lived wisely?

2. Have you loved richly?

3. And have you served the world greatly?

If these questions are important at the end of your life, why not have the personal courage to make them important now. Elite performers are simply people who have discovered what is most important to them in their lives and then built their days around these priorities. Carve out a silent period for yourself over the coming week and reflect/journal on the "final questions" stated above. Clarify what living a wise life means to you. It may mean treating others well, showing up at your best and seeing a blessing in every adversity. Then reflect on what loving richly through the course of your life means to you. Does it mean being vulnerable and speaking your truth in relationship to everyone in your life? It may mean practicing daily acts of compassion, understanding and forgiveness. It might simply mean taking the time to enjoy connecting to other human beings and appreciating how good it feels when you do so. Finally, create a mental model about what a life spent serving greatly would look like. Ask yourself: "what am I doing to build the world?" Reflect on your legacy and how the generations who will follow you will know that you have graced this planet.

This little exercise will take no more than one hour to complete. Yet it will allow you to live a life that is far more intentional, deliberate and conscious.

8 WAYS TO TAKE CUSTODY OF YOUR LIFE

1. Turn wounds into wisdom. See stumbling blocks as stepping stones.

2. Rather than constantly measuring yourself against where you dream of being, appreciate how far you've come.

3. Practice the slight edge rule: each day do one small thing to improve your mind, body and spirit.

4. Understand that we see the world not as it is but as we are.

5. Focus more on creating deep value than on making the sale.

6. Know that change at work and in life is nothing more than your growth coming to get you.

7. When setbacks strike, relax and ask: "where is the life lesson here?"

8. Realize that on the other side of your fears lies your fortune.

36

THE NEED TO PLAY BIG

⊙

I RECENTLY SPENT two and a half days with a group of some of the most brave, fascinating, evolved, passionate and loving human beings I have ever met. This band of dreamers came from around the world to attend The Awakening Best Self Weekend, our flagship personal discovery weekend that has helped thousands of people live their best lives, personally and professionally. One of the world's top children's show producers attended from Australia. A Nobel Peace Prize nominee attended from South America. CEOs and entrepreneurs participated alongside homemakers, students and teachers drawn from America and Canada. All came for one simple reason: they knew in their hearts that a bigger life was available to them and they had the boldness of spirit to act on that knowing.

Over the weekend, I observed ordinary men and woman showing up as extraordinary. I saw a group of human beings having the courage to look deep within themselves to discover their best as well as bring awareness to the constraints that limited them for most of their lives. I watched them first embrace, then transcend their dominant fears and reconnect with the sense of childlike wonder that so many of us have lost as we have left the perfection of childhood and matured into overly serious and jaded adults. Remember, adults are nothing more than deteriorated children. The goal, I believe, of this human journey through our days is not self-improvement; it is self-remembering. Finally, I watched them laugh and even cry as they arrived at the realization that personal greatness is not reserved for the chosen few. It is the birthright of every person walking the planet.

These people, and you, are my heroes. Sometimes the demands on me make me weary. But when I watch individuals such as those I saw at The ABS Weekend or meet people at my seminars who have taken personal responsibility for the way their lives look or hear stories of people who have read my books and taken the information to play a much bigger game as a human being, I get inspired. Too many people are playing small with their lives. Too many people are betraying themselves by operating at a level far below their capacity. Too many people have stopped believing in their once tightly-held dreams and passions. And this has happened because good people have forgotten that they were meant to be great. They bought into the fears of those around them and resigned themselves to mediocrity.

Let me ask you a question: what would our world look like if everyone was playing at their highest and best, loving their work and their lives in general? We both know the answer to that. So start today, as an army of one. Shed the shackles of your past and be more imaginative, more excellent, more positive and more loving. Be the person you know in your heart you have always wanted to be. Play better, bolder and bigger. I dare you.

INSPIRATIONAL QUOTES

"Human beings are powered by emotion, not by reason."

Kevin Roberts, CEO of Saatchi and Saatchi

"Respect is love in plain clothes."

Frankie Byrne

"The place where your greatest fears live is also the place where your greatest growth lies. Why would you ever run away from that?"

Robin Sharma

QUESTIONS TO JOURNAL ON

1. What is the single best lesson life has taught you?

2. Who would you be if you did not know who you were?

3. What does greatness look like in your life?

4. If an 18 year old asked for your finest advice on life success, what would you tell her?

5. How will you feel at the end of your life if you do not make the changes you know you need to make?

THE PERSON THAT THINKS THE MOST WINS

Over the past years, I have had the privilege to serve as the success coach to some of the most successful people on the planet. I have worked with leading CEOs, wildly successful entrepreneurs, a five-time world speedboat racing champion and some stars who wanted to find a better way to live. If there is one trait I have observed amongst those who live extraordinary lives it is that the best of the best make the time to think. Too many people are asleep at the wheel of their own lives. Too many people are living their lives by accident. Too many people are so busy running through their days that they do not think about where they are going and why they are running. Here's a powerful formula I share with my coaching clients: spend a third of your time thinking (planning, evaluating, analyzing and building awareness), a third of your time doing (acting on your goals, making things happen) and a third of your time on communicating (coaching, building relationships, evangelizing around your hopes and dreams).

Get up in the morning and think. Review your plans and spot your limitations. Reflect on how you are working and living and commit to making course-corrections to get better. Think about what needs to happen during your day in order for you to feel you have lived fully and greatly. Remember, as you live your days, so you craft your life. Your days really are your life in miniature. And also remember: when you think better, you will do better.

About the Author

Robin Sharma is a globally respected humanitarian and the founder of a not-for-profit venture that helps children in need lead better lives.

Widely considered one of the world's top leadership experts, this pathblazer's clients include many Fortune 100 companies, famed billionaires, professional sports superstars, music icons and members of royalty.

Organizations that have engaged Robin Sharma to help them build employees who lead without a title, produce exceptional work and master change in these complex times include NASA, Microsoft, NIKE, GE, FedEx, HP, Starbucks, Oracle, Yale University, IBM Watson and the Young Presidents' Organization.

He is also one of the most in-demand keynote speakers in the world. To inquire about his availability for your next conference, visit robinsharma.com/speaking.

The author's #1 bestsellers, such as *The Monk Who Sold His Ferrari*, *The Greatness Guide* and *The Leader Who Had No Title*, have sold millions of copies in over 92 languages, making him one of the most broadly read writers alive today.

For more information, visit robinsharma.com

Fuel Your Rise by Reading All of Robin Sharma's Worldwide Bestsellers

Have you ever noticed that the most thoughtful, articulate, success-ful and graceful people you've met all have a common practice? They read everything they can get their hands on.

Whether you're at your mountaintop or just starting your climb, reading is one of the masterhabits of the great ones.

So here's a complete list of the author's internationally acclaimed books to support your ascent into peak productivity, total craft mastery and living beautifully—while you make your mark on history.

[ ] The 5 AM Club

[ ] The Monk Who Sold His Ferrari

[ ] The Greatness Guide

[ ] The Greatness Guide, Book 2

[ ] The Leader Who Had No Title

[ ] Who Will Cry When You Die?

[ ] Leadership Wisdom from The Monk Who Sold His Ferrari

[ ] Family Wisdom from The Monk Who Sold His Ferrari

[ ] Discover Your Destiny with The Monk Who Sold His Ferrari

[ ] The Secret Letters of The Monk Who Sold His Ferrari

[ ] The Mastery Manual

[ ] The Little Black Book for Stunning Success

[ ] The Saint, the Surfer, and the CEO

WHAT'S NEXT FOR YOUR HIGHEST SUCCESS?

Nothing transforms until you move. To ensure you experience real results, Robin Sharma is making available a potent online resource that will help you think like a titan and perform like a pro.

Go ahead and get full access to it before this offer ends at:

TheMentalMasteryToolkit.com

JAICO PUBLISHING HOUSE

Elevate Your Life. Transform Your World.

ESTABLISHED IN 1946, Jaico Publishing House is home to world-transforming authors such as Sri Sri Paramahansa Yogananda, Osho, the Dalai Lama, Sri Sri Ravi Shankar, Sadhguru, Robin Sharma, Deepak Chopra, Jack Canfield, Eknath Easwaran, Devdutt Pattanaik, Khushwant Singh, John Maxwell, Brian Tracy, and Stephen Hawking.

Our late founder Mr. Jaman Shah first established Jaico as a book distribution company. Sensing that independence was around the corner, he aptly named his company Jaico ('Jai' means victory in Hindi). In order to service the significant demand for affordable books in a developing nation, Mr. Shah initiated Jaico's own publications. Jaico was India's first publisher of paperback books in the English language.

While self-help, religion and philosophy, mind/body/spirit, and business titles form the cornerstone of our non-fiction list, we publish an exciting range of travel, current affairs, biography, and popular science books as well. Our renewed focus on popular fiction is evident in our new titles by a host of fresh young talent from India and abroad. Jaico's recently established translations division translates selected English content into nine regional languages.

Jaico distributes its own titles. With its headquarters in Mumbai, Jaico has branches in Ahmedabad, Bangalore, Chennai, Delhi, Hyderabad, and Kolkata.

SINCE 1946